Moving On

Remembering My Turbulent Years
1919-1948

Moving On
Remembering My Turbulent Years
1919-1948

Eleanor Hinig Davies

Three Sons Press
New York - Washington, DC - Providence
2019

COMMEMORATIVE FIRST EDITION

Cover Photo: Eleanor Davies in front of Newton Memorial Hospital, Cassadaga, New York, a tuberculosis sanitarium where she was successfully treated, 1947-1948.

A Morning Prayer

Oh God—there are choices that face
me today
And I need your guidance to turn
the right Way
And grant me the Grace and the Wisdom
to know
When to hold on and when to let go.

- Eleanor Hinig Davies

Contents

Cast of Characters

Preface

Prologue   A Season for Tears: 1
                Reflections from Newton Memorial Hospital,
                Cassadaga, New York

PART I: DADDY (1919-1936)

1   The Innocent Years   7
        2545 Wellington Road, Cleveland Heights, Ohio
        3116 Fairmount Boulevard, Cleveland Heights, Ohio
        *("The Wellington House")
        2959 Fairmount Boulevard, Cleveland Heights, Ohio
        ("The French House")

2   Other People's Houses   29
        18700 South Woodland Road
        2970 Broxton Road and 2957 Sedgwick Road, Shaker
        Heights, Ohio (The "Twin" Houses)

3   "Goodbye, Everyone"   43
        17300 South Park Boulevard, Shaker Heights, Ohio

PART II: MOTHER (1936-1941)   49

4   The Club Residence   51
        2718 Edgehill Road, Cleveland Heights, Ohio
        "Weagle Inn," Providence, Rhode Island
        17300 South Park Boulevard, Shaker Heights, Ohio

5   With Grace   73
        Hanna House, University Hospital, Cleveland, Ohio

PART III: JOE (1941-1944)

6   Love Match   81
     The Shaker Square Apartment, Cleveland, Ohio

7   Camp Follower   93
     Army Habitats

8   The Long Road to Meadville   101

9   Sunset   105
     435 Sunset Drive, Meadville, Pennsylvania

10   How Can Emptiness Feel so Heavy?   111
     435 Sunset Drive, Meadville, Pennsylvania
     (Continued)

PART IV: LEW (1944-1948)   115

11   Healing on Water   117
     The Cottage at Conneaut Lake
     The Digs at Daytona Beach, Florida

12   Sparks Flying   127
     435 Sunset Drive, Meadville, Pennsylvania
     (Continued)

13   Cure Hour   137
     Newton Memorial Hospital, Cassadaga, New York

Afterword   153

Acknowledgments   159

Cast of Characters

Part I. Daddy
Grace Adelaide Singletary Hinig (Mother), Ellie's mother
Benjamin Calvin Hinig (Ben or B.C. or Daddy), Ellie's father
Eleanor Curtis Hinig Bainer Davies (Ellie)
Ruth Hinig, Ellie's sister
Howard C. Hinig, Ellie's brother
Alice Stanton Hinig, Howard's wife
Laura Singletary Goodhue (Auntie "Lor"), Grace Hinig's sister
Dorothy Howe Lamprecht (Mrs. Lamprecht), Grace Hinig's friend
Betty Lamprecht Slobey (Betty), daughter of Mrs. Lamprecht

Part II. Mother
Joseph E. Bainer (Joe), Ellie's first husband
Otelia Fox Bainer ("Momo"), Joe's mother and Ellie's "second mother"
John D. Bainer ("Popo"), Joes' father and Ellie's "second father"
Mary Bainer Griggs DeArment ("Mimi" and "Meem"), Joe's sister and Ellie's lifelong friend
Nancy Griggs Norman, Mimi's daughter

Part III. Joe
David Calvin Bainer (Dave), Ellie and Joe's (and Lew's) son
Liz Williams, wife of John Williams and Ellie's fellow "camp follower"
Janet and George DeArment, friends of Ellie who lived at the base of Sunset Drive

Part IV. Lew
John Llewellyn Davies, Jr. (Lew), Ellie's husband for 56 years
Bill DeArment, husband of Mary Bainer DeArment and brother of George DeArment
Bill and Jeanette Williams, friends of Ellie and Lew
Jim and Eleanor Nichols, close friends who initially knew Lew and Ellie separately from Allegheny College and the "Club Residence"

Eleanor (Ellie) Davies signs a book of her poetry at a book party in 2006.

Preface

Eleanor Curtis Hinig Bainer Davies—better known as just Ellie, Mom, or Grandy—wrote this memoir for her friends and family and distributed it in word-processed form in December, 2010, at age ninety-one. She had been working on it for decades; I have a letter from her in 1990 describing how she was still "embellishing" her life story by taking a course at a nearby college. Originally titled *Places and Faces*, the work ends at her fiftieth birthday. It received rave reviews!

Although she wrote these recollections primarily for her inner circle, Ellie was better known in her community as a poet—a talent she didn't discover until she was in her fifties. While volunteering to mentor a teenage probationer, she found poetry to be a powerful way to connect and share with this troubled young woman, who wrote poetry herself.

And the practice stuck; she continued writing poetry about her many trips, family members, and even in birthday greetings to friends. The family published several volumes of these poems—the most recent, which she titled "New Beginnings," was released on her ninetieth birthday in 2009.

It was not until I was going through my mother's office in 2017, after her death at age ninety-seven, that I fully realized how much other writing she had done as well. Detailing in particular her early years through the Great Depression and World War II, this exceptional archive told a compelling and courageous story about the coming of age of this remarkable woman who would later become my mother, a story that the family felt surely deserved a wider readership.

Because of her talent for detail and prose, there is very little text that has been significantly edited from my mother's original memoir—though I have reorganized several chapters and added new material from her extensive collection of journals, poetry, photographs, speeches, and other short works and letters, which she vigilantly kept and often shared with others. The narrative structure—which she organized around all the places she lived from 1919-1948 (which number nearly twenty!)—remains the same.

One major addition is an excerpt from a long letter she wrote to my brother Dave, detailing her first marriage to his biological father, Joe Bainer. She had written about Joe in her memoirs, but never with such emotion and specificity. After over thirty happy years of her second marriage to our father, Lew, Ellie wanted Dave to know "what life was like during the years I knew and loved Joe. I am relinquishing these memories to you to do with what you wish." Even then, it was not easy for her. She continued in her letter to Dave, "I have opened the door to the past, relived it, and gently closed it again—this time for keeps." Indeed, it was this hardy, forward-looking attitude, and an enduring openness to new beginnings, that sustained my mother through a series of trials and tragedies that surely would have led many to lose hope.

Another addition to her original memoirs is an excerpt from a speech she gave at the Cleveland Clinic about her experiences with tuberculosis. Our father's pulmonary doctor was fascinated with her recollections of how her TB was treated in 1947-1948 and asked her to speak at an annual conference.

With my brothers, Jack Davies and Dave Bainer, and extended family, we are honored to release this book in celebration of what would have been Ellie's 100th birthday. Though the many details she shares in this book evoke an era that is long gone, the lessons of life that Ellie learned through these very difficult years, which are so eloquently detailed in these writings, are timeless and have much to teach us about resilience, love, and the families we choose.

Stephen C. (Steve) Davies
September 30, 2019

Prologue

A Season for Tears: Reflections from Newton Memorial Hospital, Cassadaga, New York

Newton Memorial Hospital, Cassadaga, New York (*Reed Library Special Collections, Fredonia, New York*)

October, 1947:

"Cure Hour is over," announced the rustling nurse as she opened the door to my room that first day at the sanitarium in October of 1947. When I had been admitted an hour before, all had been quiet on the floor. But now I hear it... the *coughing*. This dreadful sound echoing down the austere corridor brought home to me the ugly truth. I had tuberculosis.

As I lay there, I tried to reconstruct my life's happenings that had culminated in that narrow hospital bed in that bare little room. Maybe the brilliant Dr. Liang—who was born in China and undoubtedly familiar with both Eastern and Western medicine—had been right when he spoke so kindly during my admission interview. Maybe too much *had* happened to me in too short a time. Perhaps I should have expressed the grief that had accompanied the events of the past ten years. In my mid-twenties, and not unfamiliar with the Bible, why had I not heeded the Ecclesiastical admonition that for everything there was a season, a time for laughter and a time for tears? Throughout this tumultuous last decade, had I allowed myself any time for real reflection?

I thought about "Daddy," still using the childish name I called my tormented father. We never shared the closeness of a daughter and a Dad. Had I felt guilt when it was too late to show him loving concern and affection after he committed that half-brave, half-crazed act of leaping from his Cleveland office window ledge seven floors to the city sidewalk below? I tried not to think of it. Besides, sixteen-year-olds have other things on their minds.

And there was Mother—my courageous, wonderful mother who kept her shoulders straight amidst this tremendous loss as she uncomplainingly faced the future without tears or self-pity. Ah, that's the way to be, I thought admiringly of my role model. How was I to know that the aching loneliness hidden behind her smile would eat away at her insides so much that within five years she would lie dying in a Cleveland hospital with only weeks to live. She had only gone in for tests.

It was April of 1941. I was comforted by a young man—Joe Bainer—with whom I'd fallen in love. I remembered when he flew to Cleveland from his Army barracks in Tennessee to comfort me and visit Mother in the hospital.

Through all of this, I could not cry on my older sister Ruth's shoulder because she kept insisting that *I* was the strong one; she needed to lean on *me*. Somehow the dreary months passed as the two of us moved from the big house to a tiny apartment while my secretarial salary sustained us.

Now my mind wandered to thoughts of Pearl Harbor. The National Guard sent all available units to guard the coast of California where dummy, wooden gun emplacements were all that existed to halt the Japanese invasion, which was believed to be imminent. Then, Joe was sent to Officer School in Kansas, followed by our July wedding and a joyful departure from Cleveland for a year of life on army bases in Missouri, the Arizona desert, and California here an inexperienced, fumbling, and naïve mother was blessed with a baby son.

In August, 1944—eleven months after Joe was shipped out to the Pacific—the telegram came saying "KILLED IN ACTION," and the feeling of emptiness that had been nagging at me became a permanent condition. But there was no time for tears. I had moved to Meadville, Pennsylvania, to live for the duration of the war with Joe's loving parents, and their hearts were broken to have lost their only son. They needed me, and they needed baby David. "If Ellie falls apart," their words echoed in my head, "we don't know what we would do." So I didn't.

Sure, there were muffled sobs in the night that baby David couldn't hear. Or sometimes in the shower. But they were not enough to relieve the hurt—so I could always clean the basement or practice the piano for the lessons I began taking to fill the time I used to spend writing letters overseas.

One night after the war, the world suddenly seemed a bit brighter after I'd had my first date with a returned Navy man. He was handsome and intelligent, and we talked far into the night. As I saw the warm expression in his brown eyes one evening when David tiptoed into the living room in his nighty-nights, I knew here was a man who loved children and family—and who someday would love me.

Springtime and summer passed and I learned to love this deep-voiced Lew (Llewellyn) of Welsh descent. We saw each other every night. I arose early in the morning with David and kept books on a volunteer basis for a thrift shop. That was why I was so tired, I thought. But why can't I shake this maddening cough?

Suddenly I found myself jolted back to the reality of that hospital room to find tears streaming down my cheeks and the seed of a thought beginning to sprout in my mind. *Could this sickness be a gift?* Already I had spent more time contemplating my life than I ever had, turning back layer by layer the defenses and walls I had built to cover the memories of the past.

The words came to me: *He maketh me lie down in green pastures; He restoreth my Soul.*

I sat on the side of the bed, noticing for the first time the bright blue October sky outside the window, and marveled. There must be a reason for my being sick. After I have grieved properly and wept healing tears, I will put the past behind me where it belongs, and emerge from this place renewed, refreshed, healthy, and full of joy for life.

And I did.

PART I. DADDY (1919-1936)

Daddy

The click of my father's
walking stick,
staccato to match
his spatted feet;
my little legs trying
to keep up
in my flashing
patent-leather shoes;
never quite fast enough,
fast enough or anything
enough.

- Eleanor Hinig Davies

Chapter 1. The Innocent Years

Eleanor Curtis Hing as an infant.

The house on 2545 Wellington Road, built in 1915 by Benjamin Hinig.

September, 1919:

On Tuesday, September 30 at 1:30 p.m., Eleanor Curtis Hinig, an eight and one-half pound baby girl, was born to Grace Singletary Hinig and Benjamin Calvin Hinig at Mt. Sinai Hospital in Cleveland, Ohio. It was almost a year after the Armistice of World War I and Woodrow Wilson was President. It was just in time for the heyday of the twenties.

Mother liked the name Eleanor, and thought it would never be shortened to a nickname. "Curtis" was her Revolutionary War ancestor's name.

Having another child was not a planned event. Already my parents had what they thought was an adequate family: a daughter, Ruth, who was ten; and a son, Howard, three. My parents, though loving, enjoyed an active Cleveland social and business lifestyle. It's no wonder that when I was brought home to my nursery I was handed over to a white-haired, starch-capped "baby nurse" named Miss Kirchner, who was followed by other nurses and then a nanny until I went to kindergarten.

Baby Eleanor and her mother.

From a book called *The Beautiful Children of Cleveland*, to which prominent Clevelanders subscribed to have their children included.

Benjamin Hinig as a young man.

Before all this: Ben Hinig, a successful insurance man, had long since migrated from the rural Ohio town of New Philadelphia, leaving behind his farming, Swiss-descent parents and five older brothers and one sister. Tall, slim, well-dressed, mannerly, and humorous, he soon lost the "country" out of the "boy."

When Ben met my mother—Grace Adelaide Singletary—through mutual friends, it was no wonder he was immediately smitten, and Grace had seen great potential in this ambitious young man. She was a tall, brunette-pompadoured, and charming young woman whose father owned a thriving lumber company. A privileged "city girl," Grace had been in the first graduating class of the exclusive Laurel School in Cleveland, and then furthered her education at Washington College for Young Ladies in D.C., where she was president of her class for two years. In a treasured box, I have the dress she wore at their small but elegant wedding on October 24, 1905. (It was a wedding dress that I would later wear, too, but I'm getting ahead of the story.)

My maternal grandmother died when Mother was eleven. When her father, Anson Reuben Singletary, married Susie the housekeeper, Mother's favorite brother, Myron, left home and vanished forever, leaving an empty place in his sister's heart. Her brother, Howard, who had served in the Spanish-American war, had died when he was but thirty-four. My paternal grandfather died two years before I was born. He had obviously doted on Mother's older sister, Laura. Laura was

10

brown-eyed and beautiful, it was said, but cold and aloof in contrast with sweet, loving Grace, ten years younger—the same age difference I would share with my older sister, Ruth.

Grace Adelaide Singletary in her college
graduation dress.

But, of his two daughters, it was Grace whom Anson Singletary made Vice President of the Singletary Lumber Company, which, as a supplement to his insurance business, provided the resources for my father to launch his career as an eminent builder in Cleveland. The house we lived in at 2545 Wellington Road was in fact built by my father in 1915.

By the time I arrived, my mother had twice before performed the traditional layette preparation. She had no patience for sewing tiny garments by hand, so she surreptitiously purchased mine downtown at Halle's Department Store and snuck them into our house in Cleveland Heights, Ohio.

Gifts for my first Christmas included several rattles, a large celluloid ball, a rubber doll and my own big scrapbook—a forerunner of a lifelong collection and an enduring hobby of mine. My Baby Book was kept sketchily and sheds little light on these years, especially two blank pages entitled "Bright Sayings!"

The blank "Bright Sayings" pages from Eleanor's Baby Book.

I was told I was a sunny, social baby. My only hazy memories are sitting in my crib talking to my imaginary playmates—two girls both named Jane and one naughty boy with the not-so-subtle name, "Brudder." I have no recollections of my real "Brudder" who must have been toddling elsewhere in the house. Nor do I recall that big, older sister who was likely out playing rather than studying. My sister found me a noisy intrusion in her life; and my brother, an uninteresting one.

I vaguely remember my busy Daddy, but somewhere inside my heart are memories of Mother's soft lap as she sings me lullabies at bedtime.

My mother was tall, matronly, and carried herself with dignity; she appreciated my father's keen sense of humor. As the ultimate insurance agent, he was well-dressed, well-liked and respected in the community. Socially, they made a glimmering couple.

Although my father and his genial Irish partner, Bob Bixby, had a profitable, independent insurance agency downtown, he had also begun investing in and building grand houses in the affluent new suburb of Cleveland Heights. In all, between 1910 and 1928, B.C. Hinig and Company built 26 homes in Cleveland Heights, twelve on the Height's premier street of Fairmount Boulevard alone.

Benjamin Hinig in his prime.

According to the Western Reserve Historical Society records, in June of 1919, the year I was born, a building permit was issued to the B.C. Hinig and Company and Grace S. Hinig, Vice-President of Singletary Lumber Company, for a large brick house at 2828 Fairmount Boulevard. The idea was that we would move into this house, selling 2545 Wellington Road, and live at 2828 Fairmount until a buyer came along—while my father was building yet another house for us to move into. The architect, as with most of my father's houses, was Frederic William Striebinger, who was said to have been the first Clevelander to study at the famous architecture school in Paris, the École des Beaux-Arts.

I wasn't sure why my parents would refer to this as the "Rockefeller House," until I later learned that John D. Rockefeller's well-traveled niece, Alice M. Rockefeller, purchased it in 1924, and filled it with treasures from all over the world. Surely, such a prestigious buyer must have helped my father's business and affirmed his clear devotion to quality workmanship and design.

2828 Fairmount Boulevard in 2019. Built on spec by Eleanor's father, this house was purchased by Alice Rockefeller, niece of John D. Rockefeller.

3116 Fairmount Boulevard, Cleveland Heights, Ohio
("The Wellington House")

3116 Fairmont Boulevard. Photo taken in 2019.

Winter, 1924:

My memories actually begin in the enormous, red brick house that still looms on the corner of Fairmount Boulevard and Wellington Road, which my father had also built "on spec." To my four-year-old mind, it always seemed dark in that house. The mahogany paneling in all of the downstairs rooms was never brightened, even by sunshine or lamps. The one room I remember with fondness was the windowed breakfast room where I can still see our smiling housekeeper serving breakfast to me and nurse Frances, which often included prunes with cream and toast and butter-balls, which our cook, Mary, made with two textured paddles in the kitchen labyrinth beyond. The flowers on the table had been tended by Dutch gardener, Peter, who also took care of my father's two Studebakers.

Upstairs over the garage was the sewing room, where crotchety Mrs. Lowry would come and create beautifully beaded party dresses for Mother and more appropriate ones for Ruth and me. For dress-up occasions, I wore pretty smocked dresses and white silk stockings along with black, patent leather Mary Janes. For ordinary, everyday occasions, I wore dresses with matching bloomers that buttoned onto a panty waist. Underneath it, I wore short-sleeved, one-piece underwear with a drop seat.

The exterior of 3116 Fairmount Boulevard, c. 1926.

A detail of the lavish interior of 3116 Fairmount Boulevard, c. 1926.

During the entire winter season (which Mother thought ran from September to the end of April), I would struggle into long-sleeved long underwear, which was incredibly difficult to fold neatly over the ankles and under stockings. Being meticulous has never been a strong trait of mine!

Once a week a lady named Agnes came to shampoo and curl Mother's hair. I wore mine in long curls, brushed each morning around a cut-off broom handle. Evenings when Mother was home, I recall the warmth of cuddling in her lap as she sang always the same lullaby about the animals and birds who had gone to sleep—one that in later years I would sing to my own infants.

In those days, Mother's activities were myriad and included serving as President of Laurel School Alumni Association, as President of Fairfax School PTA, and as a member of the Shaker Heights Neighborhood Guild, the Fairmount Garden Club, as well as scores of patriot organizations like the DAR. Except for the latter, I know I have some of Grace Hinig in my genes.

During the summers, Mother traversed the perilous gravel roads to Michigan with me, my brother Howard, and the nurse. Ruth was in camp near Cedar Lodge at Grand Traverse Bay where we stayed. Daddy

"Hostesses of the White House"—given in the ballroom of 3116 Fairmount Boulevard by the "Daughters of 1812" —from an article in *The Plain Dealer*, November 23, 1924.

would stay in Cleveland where he would work at his insurance business, play some golf, and then spend two or three weeks with us in Michigan. Even there, he was not especially a presence.

Eating watermelon on the rocks in Michigan.
(Eleanor on the left, Ruth on the right.)

One year, our family returned on the D&C (Detroit and Cleveland) Steamer. I have a frightening, fragmented memory of some man (could it have been my father?) holding me over the rails high above the water. I wonder if that has anything to do with my fear of heights, which haunts me to this day.

My recollections of Howard are of a sensitive, brown-eyed boy who teased me every chance he found. In later years, I learned he had invented an imaginary person on whom he blamed every conceivable evil, whom he named "Sicker!" (as close a connection to "sister" as you're going to get). Once when Howard was ill, I had to deliver his

18

Pictorial Review magazines while Mother waited in the car. I will never forget the mischievous December afternoon when we two accidentally shared the revelation of Santa's hiding place for a fire engine and a big doll.

"Sicker" and "Brudder."

Christmases were extravagant and jolly, usually shared with some close maiden lady friends of Mother's whom we called "Aunties." One year, for her son, Mother acquired a German Shepherd named Gretchen who was claimed to be an offspring of Strongheart, the current movie dog and forerunner of Rin Tin Tin. Gretchen soon became Mother's pet. Every night, she slept on a blanket outside my parents' bedroom door, and every morning she was fed breakfast with baby talk.

As my sister Ruth would later tell me, in Cleveland during these heydays, my father was regarded as prosperous, affable, and well-dressed—spats and all. My handsome father was uproariously funny when times were good. In the days when he built those spectacular homes, he golfed at the Shaker Country Club and lunched downtown at the swanky Mid-Day club with other affluent businessmen of Cleveland.

This is the father that Ruth remembered. Her version of the story was that he was particularly attentive to her, often taking her to the Mid-Day Club on Saturdays for lunch. Ten years younger, I guess I hadn't noticed, or wasn't noticed.

At home he had mood swings, but in the Wellington house, usually Daddy was witty, a punster, and a mimic. In addition to his extensive real estate holdings and his insurance business with Bob Bixby, Daddy was a Mason, Director of the Children's Fresh Air Camp, trustee of the Fairmount Presbyterian Church, and he belonged to both the Shaker Country Club and the Union Club.

Ruth was popular, funny, wild and rebellious—a Jazz Age flapper whose boyfriends roared in and out of our driveway in shiny roadsters or their fathers' touring cars. She attended Mother's alma mater, the private all-girl Laurel School, from which Mother was a member of the very first graduating class. Ruth hated Laurel, schoolwork in general, and anything else that didn't have to do with boys. She had short hair, short skirts, and a short temper.

The three years of my real childhood were spent in the Wellington House, but when Daddy's "French House" was completed, it was time to move three blocks away.

2959 Fairmount Boulevard, Cleveland Heights, Ohio
("The French House")

2959 Fairmount Boulevard. Photo taken in 2019.

February, 1927:

Also designed by Frederic William Striebinger, and designated in 1976 as part of the Fairmount Boulevard Historic District, this residence—known in our family as "The French House"—has been described as "elegance in stucco." With its French provincial woodwork everywhere, the house listing, eighty years after it was built, pointed to its "Beautiful oak floors on all three floors; Library and Garden Room on the first; Custom Kitchen Butler's Pantry and Breakfast Room; private fenced yard with porch and patio; and Ballroom on the third floor."

It must have run way over construction costs, and even with the money from the sale of The Wellington House, I look back and wonder if this dream house of my Father's didn't actually turn into a nightmare. For Mother, too, as she had co-signed everything.

It was 1927, and change was in the air. Young as I was, I could still feel it. No more Joseph or Mary or Frances or Peter. At the new house on Fairmount, they would be replaced by minimal staff. It was probably not a good sign that Daddy started advertising for clients. The ad also mentions that he is "now constructing" a number of "very attractive homes," surely straining his resources.

WILL BUILD LARGE FRENCH TYPE HOME

B. C. Hinig Buys Site on Fairmount; Ex-Gov. Davis Sells House.

BY J. G. MONNETT, JR.,
Real Estate Editor.

B. C. Hinig who has had constructed and sold a large number of the high class residences in the Fairmount boulevard section of the Heights, yesterday had work started on another large house which will be unusual in design and planning.

This house will be of French type and will contain sixteen rooms, a large ball room and five baths. It will be constructed of cut stone and stucco and its high French roof will make it distinctive in the neighborhood. All doors and windows, which of course will be of the French type, will be of steel. F. W. Streibinger is the architect. The cost will be approximately $150,000.

The site is a heavily wooded parcel on the north side of Fairmount boulevard a short distance west of the H. A. Tremaine residence at 3001 Fairmount, which recently was purchased by Michael Gallagher of the M. A. Hanna Co. for $225,000. The Hinig lot is 114 by 240 feet. It was purchased from John A. McGean for an indicated $30,000.

Mr. Hinig recently sold a large residence at Fairmount and Fairfax roads to Mrs. Frank Rockefeller and her daughter for $120,000.

The Plain Dealer, September 8, 1923.

Advertisement by Benjamin C. Hinig near the end of his building career.

As the baby in the family, I always had the bedroom nearest my parents' room. My furniture in every house was cream-colored with pink flowers painted on the headboard, desk, and dresser. The most important part of the room was the dollhouse, and it was the best thing Daddy ever did for me—having his carpenters build this grand but miniature, shingled six-room house (open to the front) in which I would spend countless hours arranging and rearranging the furniture for my make-believe family who lived there. My large doll with the porcelain face and long curls sat primly in a chair in the corner. I was an extremely imaginative child and spent a lot of time daydreaming. I was much like the girl in a picture on my bedroom wall—lying in a meadow, in a mist beyond her dancing fairies.

I had attended kindergarten at Fairfax School, and later changed to Roxboro School. In the summer, my new neighborhood friends and I played all through the days and long evenings at Kick the Can, hopscotch, jacks, jump rope and Tap the Icebox. One time playing Mumbley-Peg, I stuck the knife in the top of my foot—the first (but not the last) time I would prove to be accident-prone.

Eleanor Hinig was the tallest girl in her third-grade class at Fairfax School, Cleveland Heights, standing in the middle of the center row.

I hated the time I had to spend practicing the piano, much less enduring my music lessons when Miss Overstreet would rap my knuckles with a ruler if I did not arch my hands correctly. I could hardly conceal my relief when Mother announced I wouldn't be taking piano lessons anymore, but the reason was subduing. My father had something called a "nervous breakdown" and he was going through something called "bankruptcy."

He spent a lot of time upstairs in his room with the door shut.

B.C. Hinig's bankruptcy becomes public in a prominently displayed advertisement in *The Plain Dealer*, August 5, 1928, when his remaining vacant lots in Cleveland Heights were auctioned off.

I eked out some knowledge of the word "appraisal" as some of the rooms in the house began to look more and more bare, and as my mother began to stash away oil paintings and small Oriental rugs. One day some men rang the doorbell and on the way to answering it, Mother paused and grabbed the gold clock off the mantel and, scurrying to the kitchen, stuck it in the icebox. After the appraisers left, the clock was returned undamaged to its rightful spot.

Not all of my recollections of the French House are gloomy. Ruth and Howard (who by now had dubbed me "Rat-eye") and I used to play Anagrams and some hilarious word games. I remember the first time I made them laugh. What a delicious discovery and a moment of triumph!

My young friends and I used to put on made-up plays on the stage of the ballroom, closing the gold velvet curtains, bowing to the unseen audience. When we had first moved in, my sister's debut had been held in the ballroom and I understand my father worried all evening about the boys sneaking "hootch" up the back stairs.

Those glory years fading, at eight years old I would spend most evenings "dancing around the living room" (my favorite line from the 1970s musical, A Chorus Line) to the music on the radio. Begging for lessons, I got the same response as when I would plead for a new dress or braces on my teeth: We can't afford it.

Mother began to stay home more, and if she was snubbed by the ladies of the clubs from which she had resigned, she did not show the hurt. It was 1928 and the real estate market hit bottom (today we would say the "bubble burst") before the stock market crash of 1929; so Mother was uniquely in financial straits before the Great Depression affected the rest of her peers.

She did have one loyal and glorious friend who stuck by her through good times and bad. She was the wealthy Dorothy Howe Lamprecht, who had come to Cleveland from Kansas City and oil money. This warm-hearted, kind woman had a big influence on all our lives.

Mother learned to cook rather plain food and since she only had day help, I was given the task of drying the dishes while she washed. Next to the (nonexistent) butler's pantry, it was cozy in the big kitchen

Life in the French House

I lived in this last house Daddy would build on Fairmount Blvd from the time I was 7-9 years old; my brother, 11; sister, 18. I can remember: dancing in the living room to Victrola music; playing kick-the-can outside with neighbor kids; putting on plays with them on the ballroom stage (with gold velvet curtains); practicing the piano; drying dishes with my mother. Daddy had a "nervous breakdown" when the Real Estate Market tumbled before The Crash and he had to go bankrupt. (Bad times) Still recall how brave my mother was through this life-style changing times. I learned early "experience is what happens when you don't get what you want"

Eleanor's reminiscences of the French House written about 2004:
"Experience is what happens when you don't get what you want."

by the wooden drain board. (Sometimes I wonder when mothers and daughters *talk* in today's world of automatic dishwashers.)

We had a huge gas stove, one of the first "electric ice boxes" ever installed in a private house, and a cooler box in the kitchen window which we used when the weather suited.

One exciting day after my father was feeling better, he drove all of us down to the Art Museum where, on the steps amidst throngs of people, stood the young man who had flown alone across the Atlantic the year before—Charles Lindbergh.

What pulled my father back from the brink at this point in his life was his newly-found faith as a Christian Scientist—with Mother, Howard and me soon following suit. Howard and I attended the Sunday School; Mother, who never missed an opportunity to express herself verbally, gave wonderful Wednesday night testimonies; and my father ushered.

Daddy began to laugh a little at dinner and there was a feeling that the worst was over. But we would soon have to leave the French House—the last house we would live in that he built—and move into a big empty house on South Woodland in Shaker Heights that belonged to a friend of his. My parents had promoted the idea that houses sell better with furniture in them.

And furniture we had!

Chapter 2. Other People's Houses

18700 South Woodland Road, Shaker Heights, Ohio
("The South Woodland House")

18700 South Woodland Road. Photo taken in 2019.

1928:

Thus began a series of my moves to "other people's houses" in Shaker Heights, which is adjacent to Cleveland Heights and is equally impressive and—fortunately for the Hinigs—there were many vacant homes. How I loved the house on South Woodland. When I remember houses we lived in, this one is the most vivid in my mind, sometimes in my dreams!

It was a long, narrow Tudor style home built on a slope so that there were four floors in the back and the yard extended down to the Shaker Country Club golf course. We kept the lower section "rough," and Howard was always retrieving a treasure trove of golf balls from its midst. In the winter, coasting and tobogganing on the snow-covered hills of the golf course was made even sweeter by being able to enter our basement door afterwards for hot cocoa, and flopping down to listen to the Victrola, although I never did care much for "Mr. Gallagher and Mr. Sheen," my parents' favorite.

In warm weather I used to dance in the yard or bounce on my pogo stick in the driveway. I spent hours on my bike with two new friends who wore their hair as long down their backs as I did, not necessarily the vogue then.

The South Woodland House from the backyard, adjacent to the Shaker Country Club (c. 1928).

Of course, the move to the South Woodland house entailed my entering another school; this time it was Malvern. I was in the fourth grade with a teacher I adored, Miss Heindle, who read to us out loud from the *Trumpeter of Krakow*. My alphabetical seat-mate, Jinny Horn (next to Hinig) and I became close friends and keen competitors in class, which lasted all through High School.

I played Librarian so much that Mother was sure that would be my chosen career someday. But above all else, I preferred any kind of dramatics, though I still remember the sting of my sister's laughter at the puppet show I wrote and produced, starring my dolls, which was performed one Christmas night in the dining room of the South Woodland house.

I can draw a pretty accurate floor plan of this house and, when I close my eyes, I can visualize where the furniture was placed and feel what it was like to have that house be home. I can see Mother standing at the window in the breakfast room, gazing out in sad contemplation of whatever happened to her dear brother Myron who had mysteriously disappeared after his father's remarriage to the housekeeper. Howard went out West with two other boys that summer and she used to worry about his ratty car and having enough money.

But as for me, I didn't have a care in the world!

Ruth, Howard, and Eleanor pose for pictures in
the back yard of the South Woodland House.

Our dog, Gretchen, was hit by a car one day, and until her injured leg healed, my father carried her upstairs every night to her blanket. Finally, he realized that she would be running all day on the golf course and *still* expecting her nightly service. A couple nights of ignoring her whimpers and retiring early, leaving her to slink upstairs later on her own, cured this smart, beloved dog of ours.

Mother and Daddy with their adored Gretchen.

My mother's sister, Laura, did not get along at all well with my father. When he had money, he sent her on trips all over the globe. But after he lost it all in real estate ventures, and as she said, "caused The Depression," Auntie "Lor" came to live in an apartment on the third floor of our South Woodland house. There was so much conflict between her and my father that the situation became impossible.

The night Daddy and Mother and Auntie "Lor" had it out in the library, Howard and I silently eavesdropped at the top of the stairs. By the next week, Auntie "Lor" had moved to New York City, where she obtained a paid position as Secretary of the King's Daughters Society, and never spoke to my father again, nor answered my mother's letters. Auntie "Lor" was a bitter woman with no sense of humor and she, too, favored Ruth.

Auntie "Lor" had been divorced from Willis Maxwell Goodhue in the late 1890s, when such things were *not* acceptable, but she carried on with such overwhelming, stout dignity that no one dared question Mrs. Laura S. Goodhue's reputation. Howard used to mock her hats, including one that he said looked like the Liberty Bell. She always put "Lor" in quotation marks so there would be no mistake that "Lor" was not her proper name. Like Mother, Auntie "Lor" was also a big member of the DAR and similar groups, but she alone was crestfallen that her Singletary ancestors had "missed the boat" and she could not join the Mayflower Society.

Auntie "Lor" (right) plays cards at the Shuffle Board Club in St. Petersburg Florida on March 3, 1927, with friends from Cleveland and Princeton. Her hat does have a "Liberty Bell" shape!

Howard, the source of all secret information in the family, told me that Willis had "run off with a chorus girl." Actually, I have since learned that he had been a playwright, a press agent, and a city editor of *The Cleveland News*—definitely living the life of show business—and he married an actress who must have been that "chorus girl."

In the sixth grade at Malvern, I had Mrs. Smith, the first teacher who encouraged me in my writing. To my dismay, in the middle of November, the house was sold and we would soon be living in a house on Shaker Boulevard, in the Boulevard School District. I remember the going-away party my Malvern classmates gave me and crying as they sang a goodbye song to me. How I dreaded joining a strange sixth grade class in a new school, but to my surprise I was greeted with a very warm welcome at Boulevard. Fortunately, they were casting for the Christmas play and they needed a *tall* shepherd.

As I reflect on the various neighborhoods, children, and schools to which I had to adjust as I was growing up, it is clear that those transitions greatly influenced the way I am today. Because I was always the new kid on the block, I learned to make friends easily. As an adult, I welcome the challenge to meet new people and get to know them. Also, I have learned to treasure the friends I have made along the way. Perhaps most valuable of all, at an early age I learned to accept the inevitable and not waste energy rebelling against what cannot be changed.

Moving from one house to another became an art to my parents. Each family member had his or her assigned tasks; mine was to dust and pack into cartons all the books in our library. I never remember my mother doing a Spring Cleaning. We just moved instead. One thing I hated, though, was always having to keep my room neat because "someone is coming to look at the house today!"

The big moving van would arrive in the morning and by night, twenty rooms of furniture would be arranged, beds made, pictures hung, and breakfast food ready for the next morning. This is not to say that moving day nerves weren't rampant—especially the year Ruth shattered an electric light bulb in the strings of the Baby Grand Piano. My mother's shriek hit high "C!"

14302 Shaker Boulevard, Shaker Heights, Ohio

14302 Shaker Boulevard, Shaker Heights, Ohio. Photo taken in 2019.

1931:

Recalling that first summer in the dark Shaker Boulevard house brings back memories of Tootsie Rolls, balancing one foot in front of the other on the Rapid Transit tracks, Euclid Beach, listening to the radio, playing Michigan Rummy, and being hit on the head with Tommy Hubbard's flying bat while playing baseball in a neighborhood yard. Probably had a concussion, but who knew?

In the Fall when Shaker Junior High School started, I positively glowed at seeing all my Malvern and Boulevard School friends again. I was a good student and active in track, baseball, and, of course, dramatics. My first real boy/girl party was at Lorraine Leighton's where we had supper and then went to my wonderful Seventh Grade Dance. I tried to scrunch down and not be the tallest person there, outside of the chaperones.

That Spring I had Quinsy, an infection that gets under the roots of the tonsils (which had been removed when I was six). Mother, covering all bases, called the Christian Science practitioner and then the doctor. At the latter's recommendation, I was administered a shot of whiskey—an unusual commodity in our house. I coughed so hard I broke the pouch of infection on the side of my neck and did not have to have it lanced. That is the only childhood disease I recall, which is fortunate for a Christian Scientist!

The warmest of my childhood memories was having a room close to my parents and falling asleep at night hearing their voices in conversation and laughter. In the morning my father always drank a raw egg from a small cup and took big breaths of fresh air—lingering habits from his having had tuberculosis and being at the famous Trudeau Sanitarium in Saranac Lake when Ruth was just a baby. His lifelong charity was the Fresh Air Camp, and Mother's special interest was the establishment, along with her devoted friend Dorothy Howe Lamprecht, of the Shaker Study Club—an organization that perhaps explains my interest in Literary Clubs.

The next summer when we lived on Shaker, my parents felt they could afford the $1 a day that the Girl Scout Camp in Burton, Ohio, cost. I went for one week and ended up staying another and another for most of the summer. It was not my first camp experience: Mrs. Lamprecht had sent me to Harkness Camp one summer, where I learned to swim in Lake Erie's unpredictable surf and I was in the water so often that my braids rarely had a chance to dry out.

Another year she had paid my way at Cold Springs Camp, where I would dive into the chilly waters of an Ohio lake and swim for as long as I could stand it. But I remember best my camping days with the Girl Scouts. I learned a lot about canoeing on the Grand River, diving from a high board, and enjoying the camaraderie of the other girls. Somehow the laughter, sharing, and fun made up for tent living and all the mosquito bites.

Back at home, I found my sister to be a source of fascination as she would get ready for her many dates. I was hopelessly romantic and found her lifestyle at ten years my senior to be very exciting and enviable. I would rivet my attention as she applied makeup, jewelry, and perfume at her dressing table with the three mirrors. Then, I'd watch her don stockings, high-heeled shoes (Ruth never let her height faze her), and a stunning outfit as she strolled confidently downstairs to some waiting gentleman who would be talking with my father

Once she returned for a forgotten item and found me prancing around the room in her shoes, a dress, and a green coat with a grey fur collar. She was furious! Her temper and bad moods resembled those of my father's and I was intimidated by both of them. Also, I hated that she called me "Pollyanna," the name of a nauseatingly sweet girl in a book of children's fiction.

My father's insurance business was improving, but for extra income my mother rented out two rooms and a bath at the back of the Shaker Boulevard house to two legal secretaries who rode the Rapid with Daddy in the morning and evening. I remember Mother as being quite provoked that the one who looked like screen actress ZaSu Pitts paid my father such adoring attention. The problem was solved by our having to move to the Broxton Road house and not taking the ladies along.

2970 Broxton Road & 2957 Sedgwick Road, Shaker Heights, Ohio: ("The Twin Houses")

The houses on Broxton and Sedgwick Road had an identical floor plan but looked quite different from the exterior. Photos taken in 2019.

1933-1936:

Between 1933 and 1936, we moved three more times. When the Shaker Boulevard house sold, it was time for us to move on to another vacant house, this one owned by Cleveland's Charles Arter. A prominent graduate of Allegheny College in Meadville, Pennsylvania (the town to which I would incidentally move within a decade), Charles Arter owned many houses in Shaker Heights, most standing empty-eyed and unsold. When he heard of the successful house sales that had been generated by the Hinig family's furnishings, he asked us to move, first into a house at Broxton Road and South Woodland and then a year later into its twin, a block away on Sedgewick. Having sold both of them, the third one was on "Diamond Row," South Park Boulevard.

We lived in these three houses during my High School years. One of the first events on Broxton was Ruth's running off to Ripley, New York, to marry Mel Leypoldt. The pair would then move back into our house—not unusual for couples to do during the Depression. She and Mel were divorced six months later.

Short Eastern Honeymoon Follows Wedding on Friday

MRS. MELVIN GEORGE LEYPOLDT

Mr. and Mrs. Benjamin Calvin Hinig, 2970 Broxton Road, Shaker Heights, announce the marriage of their daughter, Ruth Chapman Hinig, to Mr. Melvin George Leypoldt, son of Mr. and Mrs. Edwin Leypoldt, 3504 Northcliffe Road, Cleveland Heights, which took place Friday.

The bride is a graduate of Laurel School. Mr. Leypoldt attended Ohio State University and is a member of Alpha Chi Rho. After a short trip east, the couple will live at the Hinig home.

The Plain Dealer, May 14, 1933.

Shaker Club to Put On Wilde Play

Miss Eleanor Hinig and Philip Knesal will play leading roles in Oscar Wilde's "Importance of Being Earnest," which is to be staged by the Shaker Heights Dramatic club in high school auditorium next Friday evening.

Miss Hinig lives at 17300

PHILIP KNESAL

South Park blvd., Shaker Heights; Knesal at 2629 Dartmoor rd., Cleveland Heights. The play is directed by Miss Helen Golden, Shaker High graduate who studied dramatics in New

ELEANOR HINIG

What *made* my high school years was belonging to S.S.S., my high school sorority. I have no recollection of what the initials stood for. We were considered the outstanding girls at Shaker—not "fast" like the D.B.X.'s and smarter than those in S.B.B. We met at the girls' homes on Saturday nights and talked a lot about ideals. The boys would come after their fraternity meetings and we'd sit around laughing and talking until the popular girls were taken home by boys. I was well regarded by them ("she's just swell"), but I always ended up going home with Eleanor Webster's father—that is, until a boy named Bob transferred into Shaker High from Shaw.

I was ecstatic when Bob started driving me home from sorority meetings, and he even asked me on some movie dates on Friday nights. He wasn't that handsome and certainly not the brightest in the class, but he laughed at my jokes and didn't seem to mind that I was tall, which I felt to be a big drawback in my teens. (Actually, I don't think I felt comfortable with my height until years later when I married Lew.) But it wasn't long before Bob developed a mad crush on lovely Ruth Thompson, an S.S.S. with long fingernails, lovely hair, and gracious ways—and I was back to riding home with Mr. Webster on Saturday nights. I had no more dates with my classmates, which meant the heartbreak of missing both the Junior and Senior Proms.

In school I was in "Q" section and in Shaker's progressive system. This meant that no member of our class would be required to take college boards, and most of my affluent classmates were college bound.

I was an A student, except for Geometry, which I loathed. Looking at my yearbook, I note that I was very active in a lot of organizations and often President of them. The Dramatic Club was my favorite and I was in plays all throughout high school, playing Madame Bracknell in Oscar Wilde's *The Importance of Being Earnest*, our senior play. The headlines in *The Plain Dealer* made me smile: "Shaker Club to Put On Wilde Play."

My outside activity was ice skating, either on Shaker Lakes when they were frozen, or, when I could afford it, the Elysium Rink where I loved skating indoors to music. All through high school, I would meet Barbara Narren and Ruth Thompson and we'd take the Rapid downtown to the movies. I had a terrific crush on Tyrone Power and kept a scrapbook of his pictures. We bought paper sheets for 5 cents on which were printed the words of all the popular songs of the day—and learned them all. We'd sing them from memory as we walked to school in the mornings.

In recalling my adolescent years, I also remember Betty Lamprecht, the daughter of Mrs. Lamprecht, sort of adopted me to be a friend to Betty, who had few of her own. Betty was overweight, opinionated, and bossy, which did not make her well-liked by her classmates at Laurel School.

Mrs. Lamprecht, on the other hand, was a wonderfully generous, funny, and outspoken woman. She and her wealthy husband lived at opposite ends of their big Marlboro Road house, and she belittled him unmercifully when they were together (which was rare). I spent a great deal of time at the Lamprechts, but what I had to trade in coping with Betty was rewarded by a number of experiences I would not have otherwise had. I see now that Mrs. Lamprecht needed us for companionship and fun. She treated us as contemporaries.

We'd go on trips in her chauffeur-driven limousine to Cedar Point, Niagara Falls, Toronto, and other charming places nearer to Cleveland such as Gates Mills and Chagrin Falls. We would dine at the Union Club or the Mayfield Country Club where Betty and I would swim in the summer—looking completely ridiculous together, a beanpole and a barrel. Together, we saw scores of movies and we rarely missed a play at the Play House or the Hanna.

And what did I wear? Betty's gorgeous, expensive hand-me-downs. What she took up in width, I needed for length and almost every time I stayed the night at her house, her mother would send me home with gorgeous soft wool or silk dresses to have altered, or suits that bespoke expensive shops where salesladies would appear with one gown at a time for the customer's approval. For birthdays or Christmas, my gifts of new clothing from the Lamprechts were always exquisite and stylish, and I never minded wearing hand-me-downs.

I learned to smoke in high school and Betty taught me how to inhale. Smoking was the thing to do in those days and we felt like movie stars. At fifteen, I even recall our having cocktails with her mother where, unlike home, there was always liquor in profusion. (Becoming generous and kinder as she grew older, Betty, unfortunately, became an alcoholic at an early age and died when she was only 50, soon after her mother died.)

And then there was George, another guy who took me to plays and concerts and affairs at Western Reserve, now Case Western Reserve University, where he was a fraternity brother of Howard's. Despite his good sense of humor, I wasn't all that attracted to him but he was willing to accept me on a just-friends basis, although I think he wished for more. When I saw him in later years as a distinguished architect, my first reaction was, "I'd forgotten you were tall!" He married a musician in the Cleveland Orchestra who, in her pictures, reminded me of Mother, whom George had always admired, probably more than me.

Chapter 3. "Goodbye, Everyone"

17300 South Park Boulevard, Shaker Heights, Ohio

17300 South Park Boulevard, the "cold house." Photo taken in 2019.

Summer, 1935:

Although we moved into the house on South Park in the late summer of 1935, I will always think of it as the "cold house." Perhaps the high ceilings or the drafty hall made me feel that way, but more than likely, it was the chilling events that transpired there.

First, Gretchen died. We buried her by the wall at the edge of our property, which bordered the mansion belonging to the Van Sweringen sisters(sisters of the developers of The Terminal Tower in downtown Cleveland and Shaker Heights). Mother, who dealt with big crises with aplomb, was inconsolable for days.

Howard was beginning his Junior year at Western Reserve and lived grubbily (Mother thought) in his Pi Kappa Alpha fraternity house. When he was home, his ancient car with the deafening muffler (or lack thereof) looked incongruous parked under the porte-cochere of that South Park Boulevard house.

Ruth and I shared a sleeping porch together and had individual bedrooms. By now, *she* was wearing *my* clothes. To this day I remember the brand-new, dusty rose crepe dress which she borrowed to wear on a date and then split out most of the side seams before I ever had a chance to have it on. Of course, our school attire was a different matter. The girls wore white middy blouses and dark skirts on Monday, Wednesday, and Friday, and colored middies on Tuesday and Thursday. Our own individuality showed in the way we pinned them in the back or the scarves we wore with them. Gradually sweaters were added and then middies went.

On my sixteenth birthday, Mother went to the expense of taking some of my friends and me to the Palace Theater to see Cab Calloway on stage. The show was a disaster: my friends were bored and restless, and I was sad that Mother had spent so much money. Mostly, however, the shows at the Palace were enthralling, with 11-year-old Judy Garland belting out songs, for example, and Big Bands swinging us into a new era of music. There was dancing, too—and we all knew how to do those slow, romantic numbers with the low dip, in addition to the Shaker Shag, a forerunner of the Jitterbug.

We knew nothing of the tragedy that was about to befall our family.

Just before the Depression dipped once again, my father had begun to invest in some downtown real estate. In the fall of 1935, as his hopes began to sink along with his finances, he became very depressed and paced a lot. To save money, we barely heated the house. I can remember playing Monopoly in the library with my brother and sister, all of us bundled in coats, when Mother came in, questioning us to see if there was any poison in our medicine cabinets.

At night, I could sometimes hear Daddy crying in their bedroom. Once, I heard him banging his head in desperation against the bathroom wall. I felt worried, frightened, and helpless.

In November my father took Howard out of college and got him a job at Sherwin-Williams, where he knew executives. I think I was more upset about it than Howard was. Christmas was gloomy that year, although we all pretended everything was the same. Mother had our photographs made and put into three individual frames, and one night I saw my father holding the pictures and sobbing. Daddy begged Ruth not to go to New York for New Year's Eve, but she was headstrong and determined, borrowed the money somewhere, and went anyway.

On January 8, 1936, I was setting the table for dinner when the phone rang. I watched Mother as she answered it, squared her shoulders, thanked the caller, and hung up. Afterwards, she called us together and said there had been an "accident" at the corner of 6th and Euclid and that my father was in the hospital.

All I know is that we were all sent to Mrs. Lamprecht's house and while there, some co-worker from my sister's office called her and read to her the headlines from the paper: PROMINENT CLEVELANDER LEAPS TO DEATH.

The front page, top-of-the-fold, article in *The Plain Dealer* the next morning was somewhat less sensational. Mother is quoted as saying that Daddy had recently told her that "if he ended it all, it would be better for all concerned."

Details of the next few days are hazy. Mother was very composed and brave, even when she learned my father had left but a brief note behind on his desk and called out, "Goodbye, everyone!" from the window ledge as he jumped from his 7th floor office window in downtown Cleveland.

Arrangements were made for the funeral, which was to be held at home. People from all walks of life came to call including his devastated business partner, the elevator operator from his office building, the Van Sweringen sisters, the businessmen friends who wished they could have "helped," and, of course, swarms of Daddy's relatives from New Philadelphia, Ohio, some of whom I was meeting for the first time.

My father was fifty-five years old.

The night before the funeral, Ruth and I heard Mother pacing downstairs and she was there for a very long time. I still feel chills when I recall Ruth saying, "You don't suppose she is going to open the casket, do you?"

Throughout the funeral and the days that followed, Mother continued to show incredible courage. I returned to high school (I was then sixteen), Howard and Ruth returned to their jobs, and we stayed on at the house on South Park well into the summer, until we heard the dreaded words once again: "We're going to have to move."

Ends Fiscal Worry.

BENJAMIN C. HINIG.

Excerpts from front page article,
The Plain Dealer, January 9, 1936.

B. C. HINIG, 55, DIES IN LEAP AT EUCLID-E. 6

Insurance Firm President Jumps From Seventh-Floor Office.

WORRIED BY FINANCES

Had Built Hotels on Avenue and Shaker Houses.

Yelling "Goodby everybody." Benjamin C. Hinig, 55, president of the Hinig-Bixby Co., leaped from the company's seventh floor offices in the National City Bank Building to his death in E. 6th Street, a few feet from Euclid Avenue, yesterday afternoon at 4:40.

His body landed several feet out from the east curb of the street and narrowly missed Miss Sylvia F. Papp, 22, of 7805 Rawlings Avenue S. E., a stenographer in the Catholic Universe Bulletin advertising office.

"And to think that only Monday night I had a dream in which a man fell off a fire escape." said Miss Papp last night.

Ross Messina, 16, of 2324 E. 63d Street, and Nunzio Marullo, 18, of 6109 Thackeray Avenue S. E., newsboys at the E. 6th Street entrance to the building, said they heard a woman scream and looked up just in time to see the body strike the street.

Mrs. Hattie E. Gross, 1432 W. 112th Street, and Miss Maleda Cummings, 1809 Olivewood Avenue, Lakewood, stenographers in the Hinig-Bixby offices, said Hinig had been alone in his office about ten minutes.

Suddenly they heard him shout, "Goodby, everybody," and looked up, in the direction of his private office, and saw him falling from a window sill

46

Decades later, I scribbled this to my father:

I'm sorry I never got to know you as you rarely talked to me except to pat me on my "pretty little head" and check to make sure my shoes were shined as brightly as yours. You always were such a meticulous man—and dapper. I was proud of how you reinvented yourself from the country farm boy to the picture and reality of the successful businessman, sure of yourself downtown and in a social world who appreciated your wit and charm, which was greatly enhanced by the lovely and devoted city girl by your side.

Mother had helped you smooth out any rough edges because she saw the potential in her handsome and bright suitor whom she had wed shortly after college, which, in the early 1900s, was unusual enough for a woman. It probably hadn't hurt that her father owned a lumber yard in Cleveland which she had inherited. Although you were in the insurance business, you were able to use your god-given gift of envisioning houses and getting architects and contractors to build elegant mansions along Fairmount Boulevard in the Heights.

I used to hear laughter coming from your bedroom at night after parties at the Country Club where you drove in your shiny Studebaker. But then one day the bubble of prosperity wildly burst. I remember you wandering the house at night and crying out, "It's gone...all gone." The house, the cars, the dancing lessons—and the laughter at night.

I would like to tell you that somehow we could have all made a different life if you'd still been with us. That it wasn't worth it—leaving us behind, always wishing you could have stayed. You had our love which, sad to say, was not enough. We could have adjusted to less, much less, which, at the end of the day, we had to do anyway.

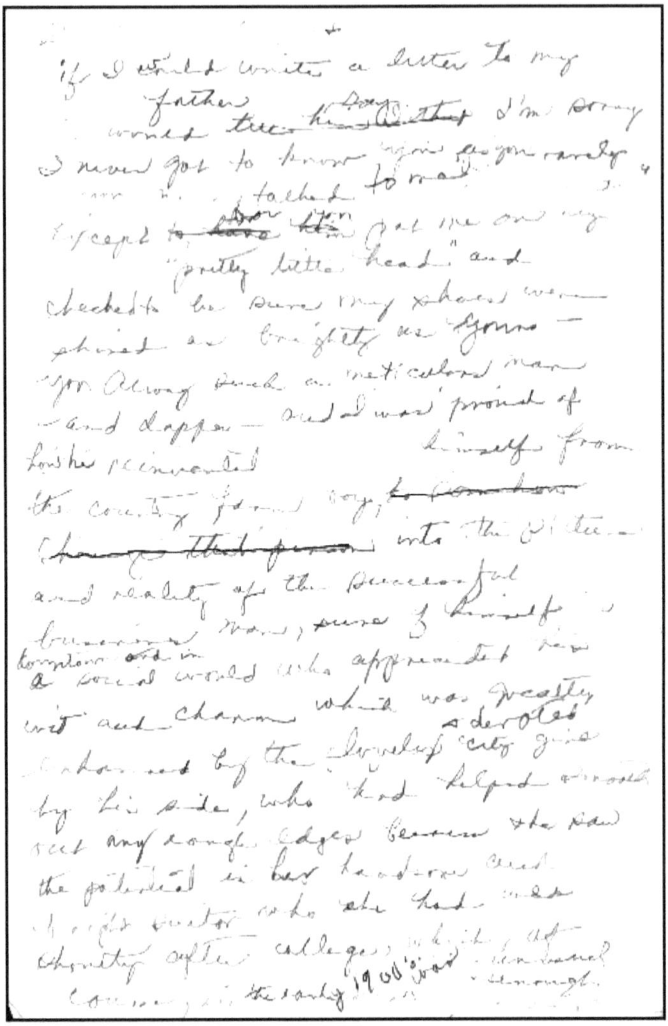

If I could write a letter to my
father
would tell him I'm sorry
I never got to know you as you rarely
talked to me
Except to pat me on my
"pretty little head" and
checked to be sure my shoes were
shined as brightly as yours —
You always such a meticulous man
— and dapper — and I was proud of
how he reinvented himself from
the country farm boy,
into the elite
and reality of the successful
business man, sure of himself
downtown and in
a social world who appreciated his
wit and charm which was greatly
enhanced by the lovely city girl
a devoted
by his side, who had helped smooth
out any rough edges because she saw
the potential in her handsome and
bright doctor who she had met
shortly after college, which at
in the early 1900's was
uncommon enough.

A portion of Ellie's scribbled note to her father.

PART II: MOTHER (1936-1941)

Mother

Soft lap and lullabies;
beaded dresses and ermine;
dignity with dimples;
inner strength
nurtured in velvet.

Aptly named Grace
she was my blessing
for when her world crumbled
her class and courage
cut the pattern
for my life.

- Eleanor Hinig Davies

Chapter 4. The Club Residence

Eleanor Curtis Hinig, high school graduate.

2728 Edgehill Road, Cleveland Heights, Ohio

2278 Edgehill Road. Photo taken in 2019.

Summer, 1936:

As the summer of 1936 began to wane, Mother knew she had to move, so she assessed our financial situation. My father had borrowed heavily on his life insurance (as had many men during the depth of the Depression) and Mother's income was scanty. Her only asset was all that furniture! In spite of having no actual business experience, her common sense led her to accept when my father's former attorney offered her the opportunity to share his family's large house on Edgehill Road in Cleveland Heights and rent rooms.

The Wilkinsons (Mr. and Mrs. and their weird son) moved into the large upstairs living room on the right-hand side of their house and Mother made a bedroom out of the opposite side of the downstairs hall, behind which were the dining room, breakfast room, pantry, and kitchen.

A center-hall broad staircase led to a large upstairs living room, and five or six bedrooms branched off the balcony that surrounded the hall. Ruth and I took one and Mother rented out the rest, including some on the third floor where Howard resided.

The problem facing me was changing school districts. Mother definitely could not afford to pay tuition until my graduation from

Shaker in the mid-year class the following February, and I couldn't bear the idea of having to switch to Cleveland Heights High School for my last semester.

Therefore, every morning and afternoon I took a bus to and from the corner of South Woodland and Lee Road, then, looking furtively around, walked to school. One day I panicked when the Dean of Girls called me into her office. She had some papers in front of her upon which she wrote my name and looked up and inquired, "Address?" I quaked inwardly and lied: "18500 South Park Boulevard." I felt relief, mixed with guilt, when she announced to me that, ironically, I was the recipient of the DAR Good Citizenship Award!

The outstanding stories of these years included Amelia Earhart being lost at sea and King Edward VIII's giving up the throne of England for "the woman I love." Romantically inclined as we were, I can still see a gang of us girls sprawled on the living room floor at Jinny Horn's, listening to his memorable abdication speech on the radio. Within days, we all parted our hair in the middle á la Wallace Simpson. My yearbook picture shows that my head looked as if it came to a point.

Eleanor (left) and Virginia "Jinny" Horn, her best friend from high school were side by side in their yearbook.

The President was Franklin Roosevelt; the French had extended their Maginot Line; and in my personal life the big news was that Ruth left home. She was a stenographer at Grasselli Chemical and when DuPont bought the company, all the employees were sent by train to Wilmington, Delaware, to live.

Mother and I moved to a bedroom on the third floor and became compatible, happy roommates. Those of us who graduated from Shaker High mid-year had skipped a grade along the way—a practice long since abandoned. For my graduation gift, she gave me a diamond ring set with one of the diamonds from Daddy's stickpin and two from a dinner ring that had belonged to her. Later, somewhere along the line, I was forced to sell it.

The Edgehill Road house was full of single men, women, and couples who were happy to find room and be in such gracious surroundings. I remember one single woman overdosed on sleeping pills because she had fallen in love with one of the married guys. She survived, but Mother vowed she would only take in single men after that. Wonderful news for me!

Mother ran the house as if it contained a large family, hiring help who cooked, cleaned, and helped her plan meals and prepare lists for the grocery store, where she endeavored to learn about buying food in quantities. I don't think that Mother ever understood how to become a businesswoman, but her determination and willingness to make a go of it were awesome. She never indulged in self-pity (a major trait of Ruth's), but looking back, I now realize how lonely she must have been at times, even though her "extended family" adored her. She never made me feel guilty, even when I didn't accompany her on her Sunday night moviegoing ritual at the Coventry Theater, a short walk from Edgehill Road.

When I was dating, she imposed no curfews or lectures on behavior, but expected me to have a code of decency and self-discipline—much more daunting than strict rules for any young high school graduate with no experience in the dating scene.

Facing reality, I realized that my going to college was out of the question financially, but I decided I would go to the best business school in the country: Katharine Gibbs. To reach that goal meant applying for a scholarship and obtaining a loan from the Miriam Kirusch Stage Fund, monies deeded by a wealthy woman who had died in the Cleveland Clinic fire in the early 1930s. Also, I would have to find a job for six months. Through Mr. Lamprecht, president of the National Refining Company in the Hanna Building, I was hired at $65 a month as a typist/file clerk in the Traffic Department.

I will always remember the nightmare of my first week there. Madly, I would file piles and piles of Bills of Lading in complete silence because, as I later learned, everyone in the eight-person office had been told that "the girl from the Heights had gotten her job through 'pull.'" After working that first Saturday morning, when I met my good friends from Shaker at the Hippodrome to see our weekly movie, I stood in the lobby and sobbed. How far away my prior life had seemed—before that dreaded, resentful-filled office. How I missed my friends who *talked* to me!

Then one day, at long last, a secretary from the office, Pat Moy, asked me to join her for lunch. Over sandwiches and a milkshake, I told her about my father's suicide. She turned pale and revealed that she had been walking past that corner at the very time the grisly incident had occurred. I don't know when she shared this information with my officemates, but from then on they treated me with warmth, respect, and affectionate kidding, which actually made it hard for me to say goodbye to them at the end of August.

Over those six months, I'd managed to save $300 since my monthly expenses for lunch and car-fare totaled only $15. Lunches cost me a quarter, plus five cents in the juke box to hear "Moonlight Serenade," and for about that much, I rode an hour each way from Cleveland Heights to 14th and Euclid on a bumpy, slow streetcar.

I had been accepted at the Katherine Gibbs in Providence, Rhode Island, where I could live in a boarding house near the school for $11 a week. However, in mid-August I received a letter from the school, awarding me only $100 toward tuition instead of the full $300 I had counted on so heavily. I remember flinging myself onto the bed in that third-floor room and weeping in disappointment. Within an hour, that blessed Mrs. Lamprecht reacted to my mother's whispered phone plea and was at our door with a check for $200 as an outright gift. My dreams were about to come true.

I had put aside some money for clothes and train fare, and Mother said she would spring for a going-away outfit. Since my father's bankruptcy, her credit was nonexistent, but ingeniously she had opened a charge account under the name of her sister at Rosenblums, an inexpensive second-floor Euclid Avenue clothing store.

So "Mrs. Laura S. Goodhue" and I went shopping. I don't remember much about the suit we bought, other than its rust color, but I'll never forget the hat! It matched the suit and had a dashing feather on the side, upturned brim. Feeling classy in that outfit—in spite of its place of origin—I boarded the train with friends headed for eastern schools such as Wellesley and Connecticut College. My sharing this experience made me feel like I belonged with the others in going East to school.

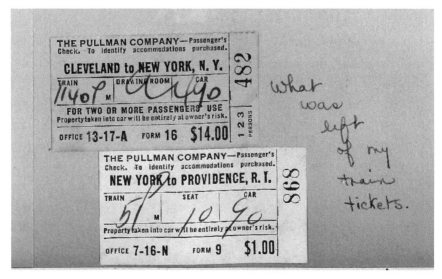

Ellie's train stubs from Cleveland to Providence, September, 1937.

"Weagle Inn," Providence, Rhode Island'

Ellie standing in front of "Weagle Inn" in Providence (c. 1980).

Fall, 1937:

On my own for the first time, I descended from the train at the Providence Railroad Station and took a taxi to the house on Hope Street where I would be staying. Plain, stout Mrs. Weagle opened the front door into the living room where we chatted a while. Mary Eaton, a boarder, told me later that she hated that person in the matching suit and hat who was so nice to Mrs. Weagle, whom she, herself, disdained. Even later, when I lived in sweaters and skirts, she never knew that my kindness to Mrs. Weagle was because I'd hoped people would treat my Mother with similar respect.

Just before school started, I gained a roommate. Martie, from Woodstock, Vermont, was my "S.S.S" kind of girl—peppy, wholesome, and full of laughter. Lynne Sigda, Dede Lord, and Betty Hatton rounded out our group. They were all New England girls, and their homes were not far away in little Rhode Island or nearby Massachusetts.

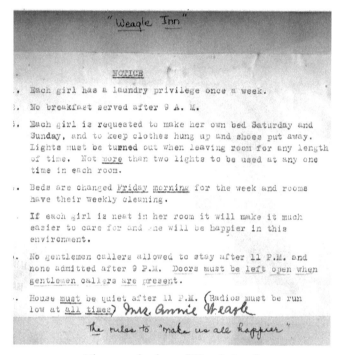

The posted rules at "Weagle Inn."

At Weagle Inn, as we called it, and at the Providence Katie Gibbs, I was considered a rarity, having come from way out west in Cleveland. I wondered if they hadn't expected lariat and spurs instead of the Rosenblum hat! The first day of school, a teacher who looked like a lovable frog read my name aloud, mistaking Miss "Hinig" for Miss "Honey," and this became my nickname from then on. The school was on Angell Street and we lived on Hope Street, which felt metaphorically appropriate. We liked to say we were "Angells" who lived on "Hope."

Learning shorthand was surprisingly difficult for me, but once I grasped it, I became very adept. With repetition comes speed, so for homework we would re-type the tests done in class. How I learned to make that old, borrowed manual Underwood sing! I enjoyed the other courses, such as advertising and office management (accounting?) given by instructors who also taught at the Boston and New York Gibbs. Sure enough, I was receiving the same excellent training as I would have at those more expensive, citified schools—and I didn't have to wear white gloves and hats to class!

"The Gang"
Mart, Lyn, Dede, Me.

The residents of the "Weagle Inn." Ellie is bottom right in the picture.

I never felt a twinge of homesickness; I had worked too hard to get there. When Springtime arrived, guys from Brown showed up in the Weagle Inn yard and hung out with our gang.

The date my roommate Martie gave me for the Katherine Gibbs dance was a lot of fun, even if I don't recall his name or what I wore. I do remember shopping in Providence one Saturday and trying on a black-and-white dotted Swiss long dress, but I couldn't possibly have afforded the $25 it cost. It's funny, but of all the dresses I've ever had in my closets over the years, the one I remember most is that one that I couldn't have! I did buy a pair of Spectators and felt very "New England" in them. I shared some apprehension about my dwindling finances in a letter to Mother, and for the last few weeks I was in Providence, Howard and Ruth each sent me $5 a week. Howard has never mentioned it since; Ruth used to remind me of it often.

Mother's letters began to sound un-newsworthy, but I didn't give them much thought. Before returning to Cleveland, I visited Martie at her family's home in the lovely White Mountains of Vermont; and then, by contrast, Ruth at her apartment in Wilmington, Delaware, where I felt ill at ease with her boyfriends. While there, I learned the reason for Mother's vague letters: she hadn't wanted to worry me, but she was planning to move, *again*.

15800 South Park Boulevard, Shaker Heights, Ohio: The "Club Residence"

The "Club Residence." Photo taken in 2019.

Summer, 1938:

Getting a job that summer of 1938 was my first priority. After a few unproductive interviews in Cleveland offices where no one had ever heard of Katherine Gibbs, Howard suggested I see Miss Ebeling, the Personnel Manager of Sherwin-Williams. There, I agreed to fill an opening in the Purchasing Department to be a "girl" for Al Millavec, and to take dictation and type purchase orders. The pay was $80 a month. I figured it was a start, and although I was surely overqualified, a job was a job in the late years of the Depression.

So on weekdays—dressed in hat, gloves, purse, and Betty Lamprecht's hand-me-down dresses—I joined the throng on the Rapid Transit, dashed through the Terminal Tower and underground hallway to the Midland Building, hopped on an elevator to the 12th floor, and headed to my desk in the Purchasing Department, which was divided by file cabinets from other department in one enormous room.

Al Millavec was a swarthy, slight, unmarried man with gorgeous eyes and horrendously bad breath. To begin with, he was uneasy with having his first stenographer, and after I stumbled over my opened bottom desk drawer to land sprawled at his feet on the first week I was there, he was confounded. It seemed to me that all calculating machines and conversation on the entire 12th floor ceased before I picked myself up and awkwardly tried to laugh off one of the most embarrassing moments of my entire life.

Just a few months earlier, in the Spring of 1938, Mother had made arrangements with Mr. Hanna, a member of a powerful Cleveland family, to move an entire houseful of our furniture into his enormous empty house on "Diamond Row" and make a kind of refined Club Residence out of it. Zoning didn't seem to be an issue. From the beginning to the end, the house on South Park—a different one from where we had previously lived—was Mother's.

Word soon spread of this elegant, sought-after place for single guys in a family setting. I hated that Howard called it a "Boarding House."

In the windowed solarium beyond a small sitting room, Mother created a bedroom for the two of us with heavy draperies for privacy, Ruth's green bedroom set, and a make-shift, curtained closet. From this cozy room, Mother would arise early in the morning and start the monstrous coal furnace in the basement, which she had banked the night before. Thinking back, I don't know how she ever managed such a terrible task until Howard took over when he moved in.

Upon entering the South Park House from the porte-cochere or another rarely-used front door, visitors would find an imposing vaulted hall framing a magnificent stairway. Along the rear of the house was a large living room with all the familiar oil paintings and oft-moved furniture, including the baby grand piano where I learned to play popular songs. I more or less mastered "These Foolish Things" and attempted "Deep Purple" and "Manhattan Serenade."

Parallel to it and at the front of the house was Mother's sitting room with a sofa bed, chaise lounge, my Hope Chest and bookcase, her desk, and the horsehair rocker where I can still see her sitting and reading, stopping long enough to greet people. Across the hall was a huge dining room, used only on special occasions, which housed the massive table, twelve lofty, tapestry-backed chairs, and a marble-topped buffet—all reminiscent of the heydays.

During the three years we lived there, that huge house with four garages was always filled with unattached young businessmen, and my popularity among my girlfriends soared. I was a one-woman Date

Bureau. Impromptu Saturday night parties would take place either in someone's suite or in a bedroom with an unusually large closet where a bar and record player could be set up and from which "In the Mood" would bellow out. I used to wonder what the guys' dates from the outside thought of coming to these gatherings, being guided through the darkened house, up the stairway and past the landing, then entering into someone's crowded bedroom and closet, alive with revelry, music, and laughter.

The "Club Residence" in 1940.

The ballroom that extended the full length of the third floor hosted many a ping-pong tournament in addition to big planned events like New Year's Eve dances and theme parties. One night, when the theme was "song title costumes," I wore a sandwich board with Hitler's picture on the front and a blue cloth "C" on the back (I was "Between the Devil and The Deep Blue Sea,") and my brother Howard, in clothes attached by pins, came as "Say It Isn't Sewed."

The informal dining room beyond the formal one was the setting for breakfasts and dinners served by household help from the gargantuan kitchen area. Even with the elongated table that Mother had made, sometimes the overflow was seated at a card table. Mother served our dinner at the end of the table and was dubbed "Gracie" by her boys, often numbering a dozen or more. To say this was a scene of hilarity and kidding is an understatement. Now called "Ellie," I was royally teased.

I learned to hand it back, but what bothered me was the feeling that Mother was compromising some of her dignity by trying so hard to be one of the crowd. To me, she always was a "Grace," not a "Gracie."

Over the years this South Park House saw a lot of boys come and go; boys who would become men in the war years that followed. I remember all their names, but I'll only tell some of their stories. I had a date one night with a guy named Dennis, who talked with Mother afterwards and moved in. He turned out to be a real jerk! Then there was Sam—a nice guy to whom I used to say "Pass the Jam, Sam" and he'd reply "Pass the jelly, Ellie." I introduced "Buck" Slobey to Betty Lamprecht and later they were married. I couldn't keep track of some of the other guys, although I did hear of some who didn't make it home again after the war.

In the summer of 1939, during my vacation in Boston visiting Martie, Frank E. Davis—Director of Purchasing and head of the Department with an office in the Executive corridor—called me and asked me to be his secretary because his "girl" was leaving. Fortunately, Howard took me aside when I returned and gave me some excellent advice about how to deal with the notoriously rude Frank Davis: "Don't let him faze you, Ellie, stand up to him." And I did, successfully at that. At least it amazed Jean Brown who, as secretary to the Senior Vice President of Sherwin-Williams, had witnessed how my boss's uncouth behavior had affected my predecessors.

Jean and I became close friends; she was more a sister to me than Ruth ever was, and the same number of years older. Jean was always there with her listening heart and a ten spot to tide me over until payday. But the loans came later. These days, I was enjoying the prestige of my new job and out of my $120 monthly salary, I could give Mother money and still pay off my Shaker High School Fund loan.

Over Labor Day weekend, Betty Lamprecht and I were with Betsy Burrows at her mother's cottage in Bertie Bay, Ontario, when on September 3, 1939, the British Empire declared war on Germany. At a nearby amusement park I still remember the scene of excited young Canadians talking about joining up, and the trembly feelings of dread I had.

That autumn I started dating Joe Bainer, who I thought was the star at the house, and life was fun and carefree when I was nineteen and twenty, and in love. I found Joe very attractive and appealing, and perhaps because I am loquacious and he quiet, we were drawn to each other. Joe was five years older than me, but had youthful good looks and a subtle sense of humor. He was a stock trader and his favorite sport was golf, where he had a natural grace. Joe had integrity.

The first time I ever saw him, Mother was interviewing him and Bob McFarland ("Mac") in the living room. The suite over the four-car garage was available and this is where Joe and Mac moved in. They had a bedroom with twin beds, a living room, and a side porch. Its most distinguishing feature, however, was an enormous closet/kitchenette. The rooms must have been for the servants and the one drawback to this suite, especially in Howard's eyes, was that the occupants had to walk through his bedroom to get there. Saturday mornings when Mac and Joe had to work and Howard didn't, there would be loud "shhhh-ing" and "Don't wake Howard!" from the two culprits.

Joe and Mac had been friends for years and were almost like a vaudeville team. Once they set up some kind of a "still" in the above-mentioned closet to make liquor. Fortunately, it didn't explode.

I remember asking Joe to go to the Sherwin-Williams Annual Dance and he asked, "With who?" then laughed when I said, "With me." I never had a better time in my younger years than at that dance, and the people from the office liked him better than any other guy I'd ever invited to those affairs; they found him fun and natural.

It was the beginning of a series of good times. When we started seeing more of each other, I complained to Joe that the only trouble was that it never seemed as if we were having a "real date." At 8:00 p.m. on a Saturday, he appeared at the front door, looking smashing in his suit and tie. One problem: he was wearing his fuzzy slippers!

We were together a lot. A bunch of us—Howard and Alice and Mac and Joe and I—always got on the Rapid Transit at the South Park station; there was a lot of laughing. Joe usually called me once a day at the office. And then there were the evenings at the house during the week and the Saturday nights parties in the ballroom or in Rus Wardley's "suite" (he, too, had a big closet). Rus Wardley was one of the funniest guys in the house but his suits always smelled of cigarette smoke.

Joe and Ellie at a "white tie" event.

Joe always was a sleepy head—known to doze off even on dates, especially if he'd had a few drinks. I called him "Sleepy Sam" after a cloth doll in PJs.

Joe joined the 107th Cavalry—the very social, blueblood National Guard outfit in Cleveland—for the darnedest reason. He had always taken vacations with Mac who drove him mad with his picture taking—the setting up of the tripod, and all. Rather than hurt his feelings, he joined the 107th so that his vacations would always be at Camp instead, and Maynard-Murch, his employer, granted him three weeks off. The plus about the 107th was that they gave fabulous picnics and dances at the Hunt Club in Gates Mills and we made good friends in the group.

Much to Mother's and my joy on Thanksgiving in 1939, Howard married Alice Stanton from Lakewood, Ohio, at Old Stone Church on the Public Square in downtown Cleveland. Alice and I were friends from the start. Mother and I said that if Howard didn't give her an engagement ring (made from the other diamond from Daddy's tie pin), *we* would. Besides, from a practical viewpoint, it was hard on our only car for him to drive to her home on Arthur Avenue, then downtown for dates, then back to Lakewood (another suburb on the opposite side of Cleveland from where we lived), then home again to the Heights.

Alice worked in the Accounting Department of Sherwin-Williams and her father was the very austere auditor of the company—that is, until one perceived the twinkle behind his British reserve. Alice was blonde, slender, and possessed a kind of serenity Howard and I lacked; hence she always has been the ideal wife for him, and friend to me.

They moved into an upstairs suite in the house on South Park where they had a bedroom, sitting room, and a shared bath. A talented seamstress, Alice brought her sewing machine with her and promised she would help me make a dress, but would not do it for me. She laughed until she cried when I accidentally stitched all the seams of a dress I was trying to make using the gatherer attachment. The garment was about fifteen inches long and I had to rip it out and start over. Obviously I was not the sewing type any more than Mother!

The nurses on duty at the hospital where Alice had an appendectomy were incredulous when the boys from the house swarmed to visit her and, two-by-two, were allowed in her room. Never did anyone have so many admirers.

In the spring of 1940, Joe drove me to Meadville, Pennsylvania, as he wanted me to meet his delightful parents, and we went to see *Gone with the Wind* at the Academy Theater. The small town was full of friendly people, none more so than the Bainers—dubbed "Momo" and "Popo" by their granddaughter, Nancy, who had moved in at the age of three while her mother ("Mimi") was in the process of getting a divorce.

Momo (bottom photo) gazes out the
huge bay window of the living room of
the Sunset Drive house in 1940,
under construction.

Ellie "walks the plank" on Sunset Drive.

Momo and Popo visit the Sunset Drive house
in 1940 while it was under construction.

On other visits, when Mimi was attending Meadville Commercial School, I would help her with her shorthand and we would talk far into the night—the beginning of a close and enduring friendship.

The Bainers were always wonderfully hospitable to me from the very first visit, when they lived on Walnut Street in the house they'd moved to from Lakewood for John Bainer's position as Vice President and Cashier of the Merchants Bank in Meadville.

On September 30, 1940, I celebrated my twenty-first birthday in the dining room of the South Park House. The butler (who also shined shoes and sometimes "borrowed" someone's car) had to climb on his hands and knees to reach the center of the table to place the floral centerpiece. Mother invited Mrs. Lamprecht and Betty, who had slimmed down, and Betsy Burrows (who was dating Rus Wardley). Howard and Alice and all the fellows completed the seatings at the gala table. Little did I know what my twenty-second year would bring!

Shortly after the first peace-time draft in history was put into motion that October—a constant topic around the dinner table—Howard and Alice moved into their own apartment on 163rd Street and somehow the house was not the same. The next upheaval was Ruth's moving back from Wilmington and taking Mother's bed while she moved to the sofa bed in the sitting room. Mother and I were easily manipulated by Ruth's aggressive nature and we both did anything to keep the peace, but how I missed Mother's and my former contented relationship as roommates.

Ruth looked around at all those young guys and settled on Bob Thompson. Attractive, shy, and naive, he never knew quite what hit him. She half-heartedly looked for a job and, of course, didn't find one.

By Christmas of that year, war news from Britain was of constant bombings and most of the European Continent came under German occupation.

We continued to have weekend parties, but Joe and I almost broke up as he sensed that he was getting so involved with me that his precious independence was threatened. Making up was worth the pain, and we celebrated by driving to Meadville to see his parents and check out how the new house on Sunset Drive was progressing.

A feeling of foreboding overshadowed the New Year's Eve party as 1940 became 1941. The whole world was changing, and my world as I had known it was about to fall apart.

Chapter 5. With Grace

Hanna House, University Hospital, Cleveland, Ohio

March, 1941:

On Sunday, March 11, 1941, Joe was inducted into the U.S. Army. At Trinity Episcopal Cathedral, the colors of the 107th Cavalry were blessed. The ceremony was witnessed by Momo, Popo, Mimi and me and a crowd that taxed the capacity of the cathedral.

This day marked the subsequent departure of the Cleveland horse-mechanized regiment for Camp Forrest, Tennessee, which was just barely finished being constructed. Before Joe left he gave me the family ring he wore—onyx with a gold "B" on it—but we made no commitments. It was the beginning of real Army life for Joe, and of loneliness for me.

Later that same month, Mother began to have some sick spells that were totally unlike her. I'd call her from the office in the morning and she'd seem alright, but after lunch she'd feel ill again. Her condition finally became so serious that our family doctor insisted she enter University Hospital's Hanna House for tests. A week later Dr. Cox shocked Howard, Alice, Ruth, and me with the news that Mother only had a short time to live—"a matter of weeks," he said. Her kidneys were so badly damaged that uremic poisoning was filling her body. The Apple Blossom Cologne I brought her from Higbee's did little to cover the odor and ruined that fragrance for me forever.

When I wired Joe, he obtained a brief furlough and flew to Cleveland. I was grateful for his loving comfort, but then he was gone again. Mother did die knowing I was going to marry Joe. He wrote her a letter after his visit, in which he said: "I'm never going to have a string of polo ponies, but I know I can make Eleanor happy." Among the last words she spoke to me were, "I have a letter I want to answer."

Her bravery and pretense when we visited her was inspiring; but sometimes she couldn't help but vomit and Howard would gently wipe her mouth. We never talked about her dying, but we learned afterwards from her nurse that she'd told her she knew she would "never get out of there" and asked if she would please help her "face the end with dignity."

One night towards the end, we were leaving and mother called me back. I stood by her bed for a long time as we communicated through our eyes. Finally she asked for some lemonade and the spell was broken. Rejoining the others waiting at the elevator, Ruth lashed out with, "Who do you think you are, the favorite child?!"

I was both hurt and resentful of her insensitivity and lousy timing. Meanwhile, where was *she* when I, at the age of twenty-one, was trying to work my job and run the house? I remember we all ate a lot of meals that included carrots and Jell-O.

Shortly after Easter in 1941, Mother died in the night. She was fifty-eight years old and had only lived five years from the time of my father's death.

At the funeral home, it was with ambivalent feelings that I gazed into the casket at Mother, never having seen a dead body before. However, she looked beautiful and much younger and very much at peace. Her hair was done wrong, but that was quickly remedied through someone Mrs. Lamprecht located.

The funeral was at home with the casket and rows of chairs in the big living room and the family in Mother's sitting room, trying not to notice the empty horse-hair rocker. I whispered, "Goodbye, I'll miss you always" at the cemetery when the casket was lowered into the ground that April day. Then huge tasks loomed ahead.

First Ruth and I went apartment hunting and located one on the third floor on 132nd Street, within walking distance of the Shaker Square Rapid Transit Station. We went through the house selecting the furniture we would take. Howard and Alice moved to a larger apartment on Bellfield Road in Cleveland Heights to accommodate some of the furnishings such as the Oriental rug on the landing, the dining room table and chairs, and so forth. The rest of the furniture we decided to put into storage. To pay some of Mother's medical bills, however, Howard sold some of the furniture and gave the remainder to charity, though not without hassles from Ruth.

MRS. GRACE HINIG, CLUB LEADER, DIES

Was Active in D. A. R. and Parent-Teachers Work

Mrs. Grace Singletary Hinig, a leader in Cleveland club work and social circles for many years, and widow of Benjamin Calvin Hinig, insurance and surety bond broker at his death in 1936, died last night at 11:45 at the Hanna House of Lakeside Hospital.

A lifelong Clevelander, Mrs. Hinig was graduated from Laurel School in 1901 and later attended the Washington College for Women, Washington.

She was married in 1905 to Mr. Hinig, who at that time headed the B. C. Hinig & Co., insurance brokers, which later became the Hinig-Bixby Co.

Mrs. Hinig was formerly active in Parent-Teachers Association Work here, at one time heading the Fairfax Parent - Teachers Association and the Cleveland Heights Council of the Parent-Teachers Association.

Active in club work, Mrs. Hinig was the organizer of the Shaker Study Club and was a member of Moses Cleaveland Chapter, Daughters of the American Revolution. She also belonged to the Daughters of 1812 Society.

Surviving Mrs. Hinig are two daughters, the Misses Ruth C. and Eleanore C.; a son, Howard Calvin Hinig, with the Sherwin-Williams Co., and a sister, Mrs. Laura S. Goodhue.

Services will be Monday at 2:30 p. m. at the late residence, 15800 South Park Boulevard, Shaker Heights.

The Plain Dealer, April 26, 1941.

Our nerves were ragged and I can't recall what she said to me that prompted my reply, with unaccustomed defiance, "If this is the way it's going to be, I don't want to live with you!" Taken completely aback,

75

Ruth sank to her knees and, hugging mine, said, "Please don't say that. You're the strong one. I need you. I depend on you." Later I learned she meant it. Fortunately, I was blessed with the aid of friends.

Jean Brown spent one whole Saturday helping me prepare to move. Good ol' Betty Lamprecht and Betsy Burrows vanished into the kitchen and pantry and didn't emerge for days it seemed. The big barrels and boxes they had packed were stashed on the fire escape of the apartment building until they had to be unpacked because they were a fire hazard. Later on, during an aluminum collection drive in the early days of the war, I think we donated enough in the way of pots and pans from the house to build a fighter plane!

The guys began packing up and moving out, some of them in a group to a lakefront estate in Bratenahl. In my mind's eye, I can still see them—one at a time, suitcases in hand and garment bags over their shoulders—coming down the stairs and past the mountain of sheets accumulating in the hall; shouting "Goodbye, good luck" as they disappeared out the door and out of my life.

Ruth was stricken with some kind of illness the day the van came so I was in charge of showing the movers around the house, pointing out the pieces we were taking, which I had tied with a string. They protested: "Lady, you can't *move* like this"—but move we did.

Before departing on top of a last load on a truck Howard provided, I took one last look around the deserted mansion. The rooms seemed to echo with youthful laughter and strains of Big Band music from now-gone record players and I cried for the times that were over, for Mother being gone, and because the future looked so bleak. By the time I reached the apartment and lugged the last lamp up three flights of stairs, I knew that I had grown up.

Easter 1991

Dear Mother,

I have very few regrets in my life, but one is that as you lay in the hospital in a coma during your last days, unnerved by the terrible sounds of your labored breathing, I sat in a room across the hall. I wish I had perched at your bedside and held your hand and told you over and over that I loved you. In recent years it has been discovered that though the patient is unconscious, the presence of another person is felt. I didn't know that in 1941.

All I knew was that at last you were slipping away from me forever. I felt a terrible sense of loss, not only of my "mommie" but of the loving person who in later years had shared, in our darkened bedroom, stories about your growing up years; what Auntie "Lor" had been like as a beautiful, but cold, young woman; and especially about your and Daddy's courtship and early married years. I wish I'd asked more questions.

Now when I think about you and the trials you endured during your lifetime, the more remarkable a woman I realize you were, Mother. The courage you showed in the face of adversity has been your legacy to me. With you as a role model, I learned that a lady gains strength from the challenges meted out to her and, grieving privately, shows the world a smiling face.

I wish now I'd gone more often to the movies with you on those Sunday nights on Edgehill. I had no conception of your loneliness. Also, you kept on being a Christian Scientist attending the new church on Lee Road long after I'd abandoned it in disillusionment when it hadn't helped Daddy at the end. I could have accompanied you more than just once—but you never expected me to and I admired your independence.

I marvel now that, after Daddy's death, you didn't just sell most of the furniture and find some small apartment and let your children find a way to support you since your insurance payments were so meager. A lesser woman would have; not my Mother, not Grace Adelaide Singletary Hinig. Instead, you demonstrated fortitude, lack of pride, and ingenuity by using the furniture as your assets and turning first one, then a second, larger house into a place for people to live and pay for their keep. (You'll notice how I still refuse to call them Boarding Houses.)

As much as I've missed you, I want you to know I am grateful you and Daddy have long been reunited.

I feel better having written this letter to you, even though, somehow, you may have known what I've expressed all along.

There will never be another you, Mother. I only hope I can live out my life in a way of which you would be proud. It has been 50 years since you died. I like to think that I learned from you that heroism lies in living, fully and joyously, in each moment that is given to us.

Your loving daughter,
Eleanor

PART III. JOE (1941-1944)

From "Thoughts at 90"

From life's arena I've memories
like home runs in last innings
of precious ones I've loved and lost
and games not always winning;
yet all goodbyes are not the end,
but only new beginnings.

- Eleanor Hinig Davies

Chapter 6. Love Match

Ellie's engagement photo, 1942.

The Shaker Square Apartment, Cleveland, Ohio

The Apartment near Shaker Square, Cleveland, Ohio.

Spring, 1941:

After mother's death, in time, Ruth and I finally became settled. Since Ruth still wasn't working, she prepared our sketchy dinners from the groceries I had bought. In addition, I paid the $55.00 a month rent (remember the $120 salary). Sherwin-Williams offered loans to employees and asked little or no interest, so I decided I would borrow $300 to cover all my bills and some of Mother's. By May, Ruth's moods had become more and more morose and somehow she convinced me she absolutely must get away. She wanted to go to Wilmington and visit awhile and have a chance to "recover" from Mother's death.

Worn down by her arguments, I finally relinquished most of my borrowed money. Cheered up considerably, she packed and left town for two weeks. I was left with bills still to pay in addition to the Sherwin-Williams' loan... a high price to pay for peace and quiet.

While Ruth was gone, I visited the Bainers in Meadville, where they were finishing up the house on Sunset Drive. The house was

Ruth and Ellie in a happier moment.

completed in that late summer of 1941 and was the only one of three houses on the street then but I think it is still the jewel of the neighborhood and it still sits facing the sunset. We were all eager for Joe to come from Tennessee to see it.

On Memorial Day weekend, arrangements were made for me to go to Nashville, Tennessee, to spend the weekend with Joe as he had a weekend pass. I stayed at the Andrew Jackson Hotel, as did Joe, in a separate room. How can I explain how different moral values were in 1941? They just were for us, anyway. We were very much in love so, of course, time sped all too fast. I returned to Cleveland on my first plane trip (on an American Airlines Flagship with props!).

In June, with Hitler sending three million troops in a massive invasion of Russia, Joe was still stationed in Tennessee, but finally a bright spot appeared in my life. Howard and Alice and I had been planning for a year to take our two-week vacation and drive out West. I don't know how I possibly afforded it, but it was an unforgettable trip and the beginning of my long-standing love affair with the American West.

From the Friday afternoon in five o'clock traffic when the three of us in Howard's car headed for Toledo, until the Sunday afternoon sixteen days later when we returned to grubby Cleveland, we giggled and gawked and delighted in every moment. We stayed in rustic cabins and ate in cheap cafes, but we were awed by the scenery of Carlsbad Caverns, the Grand Canyon, Bryce and Zion National Parks, north to Yellowstone and the Badlands. Alice and I took turns hanging out the window on the passenger's side and returned home with enviable tans.

Ellie's captions from her scrapbook of her memorable western trip with Howard and Alice in the summer of 1941:

(Above) "Ignore wild looking traveler {Ellie} and note different kinds of cactus."

"What a pleasant relief!" (Ellie and Howard).

"Ellie and Alice on a rock near Mt. Rushmore, South
Dakota. I am glaring because I asked him (Howard) not to
take the picture."

Ruth was less than civil upon my return and I used to daydream
about how nice it would have been to live with Howard and Alice
instead. Joe had another furlough in October and we spent part of it in
the completed house on Sunset Drive with his family. That
Thanksgiving I choked down dinner at Shaker Tavern with Ruth and
Auntie "Lor"—the first time I'd ever eaten out on that special family
day, but not the last.

Living with Ruth wasn't all bad. She could be very funny and even have times of genuine thoughtfulness, like when she hid a wrapped box of earrings under my pillow at Christmas. But when there was no man in her life, she could be unbearable and full of self-pity. "Everything Happens to Me" was not only a song title of the day—it was her well-used expression. Thinking of it even now sets my teeth on edge.

Finances were an ever-present problem for me in the year or so I lived with Ruth. Before every Christmas, zesty Mr. Cook of Cook Paint and Varnish in Kansas City would breeze into our office of Executive Secretaries and give out hugs, a pinch or two, and generous gifts. In December, 1941, I sold the bottle of Channel No. 5 he gave me to the perfume buyer at Higbee's (valuable because of the war) and with the money bought a good pair of black shoes. Betty Lamprecht's gift of a pink Sloppy Joe sweater—popular at the time with college girls—I exchanged at Halle's for a soft, flannel blouse and wool skirt, more appropriate for the office.

I did *have* to buy stockings to wear to the office. Nylons were still available then and had seams up the back that were hard to keep straight. Other necessary purchases were bridesmaid dresses. In and outside of the office, many of my friends were getting married and I was maid-of-honor for Betty Lamprecht's "rainbow" wedding. The fuchsia dress, which contrasted breath-takingly with the pastel ones and went well with my dark hair, was provided by Mrs. Lamprecht.

On Sunday, December 7, 1941, Ruth and I were eating dinner at Clark's Restaurant at Shaker Square when the radio blared the horrible news that the Japanese had bombed Pearl Harbor. I knew that meant that Joe would be shipped out.

A week later, a group of girls who went with guys in the 107th assembled at the Terminal and went by train to Tullahoma to say "good-bye" as our fellas were being shipped out the next week. My sister called the office and lied to my boss about my having a terrible cold and laryngitis. I *did* feel sick when I saw the supply trains being loaded with jeeps and tanks and large guns in Tullahoma, and Joe and I clung to each other for the brief time I was there. Fortunately, the supply trains were wrecked en route to the west coast, or the 107th would have shipped out to the Philippines. As it was, they stayed at

Fort Ord, California, where wooden gun emplacements lined the Pacific beaches, black-outs were in order, and the Japanese were expected to land imminently.

Joe and I wrote each other every day, but outside of letters, life was gloomy and sad and scary, especially listening to the war news on the radio every night. Everyone was glued to the radio, feeling helpless and patriotic, and we almost immediately began to rally around a common cause.

Joe Bainer, in the Army now.

Daylight Savings Time was established for more productive hours. Each wintry, dark morning and evening after work, I found the Terminal Tower railroad station had become a scene of long lines of inductees headed for army camps. Young men talked of nothing other than which branch of the service to join and how soon they could leave. Offices and factories were emptied of men and soon replaced by women working in unfamiliar fields.

Amidst all of this, one day I summoned the nerve to announce to Ruth that she just *had* to find a job, any job, or I was leaving. She cried about "ending up in the poor house" and other such dramatics, but somehow I held my ground. She *did* go out and find a job with an accounting firm downtown. She complained constantly about her back, how tired she was, how inadequate the pay was—but she stayed.

Soon after on a wonderful Spring day Joe wrote and said he was being sent to Officers Candidate School in Fort Riley, Kansas, would graduate in July, and would I marry him?! Momo selected the rings at Wood & Stone's in Meadville and sent them to him, and he mailed me my engagement ring, assuring me that he would put it on my hand properly and in person when he came home for our wedding.

Happy times began. We set the date for July 20, 1942, and I decided I would wear my Mother's wedding dress and Ruth would wear one of the bridesmaid dresses that I had worn at the wedding of a friend at the office. Ruth was to be my only attendant and Howard would give me away. Auntie "Lor" came up with payment for the church (Fairmount Presbyterian Church). After a long search, I finally found a pair of white ballet slippers. Momo went over every inch of my mother's dress with a cleaning powder, especially where the hem had to be lengthened. Also, she made a little dress for Joe's niece, Nancy, out of the same shade of dusty rose lace and net.

Mrs. Lamprecht said she would hold a small wedding reception at her home just for family and close friends—and all was in readiness for Joe when he arrived in Cleveland the morning of the wedding! That night, we were married at 8:00 p.m. in what was called "an Open Church Wedding," although I had written hand-done notes to friends of my parents inviting them to attend and sent out announcements afterwards.

Official wedding portrait.

Ruth, Joe and Ellie, Popo and Momo, Nancy in
foreground.

Momo embraces Joe while Ellie reaches out to Popo.
Nancy and Ruth (left) and Howard (right) look on.

The apartment was full of wedding presents—lots of silver-plated serving dishes, and the complete pattern for eight of Spring Glory by International. Both the Kirkpatricks and the Gilberts (friends of Joe's parents, from Meadville) drove over for the wedding.

Mrs. Lamprecht gave a lovely reception at her house for the out-of-town guests. I remember Auntie "Lor," a lifelong teetotaler, scooting around trying to avoid the waiter with the tray of Champagne. Undoubtedly she still regretted the end of Prohibition.

The photographer who took our pictures both at the wedding and in our "going away outfits" remarked that we looked like brother and sister. That's a "love match," I've heard since.

After departing in a shower of rice, Joe and I nostalgically went to the former "Club Residence" on South Park where we had met and left the rice there among our memories. We spent our wedding night at the Hotel Cleveland. The next day we drove to Granville, Ohio, where Joe had gone to Denison University, and we stayed at the Granville Inn for our honeymoon. It was a heavenly time which included lots of long, long talks as we had a lot of time to catch up on. The last few days of our honeymoon we spent in Meadville, then said goodbyes again until Joe was given his next assignment. I returned to the office awaiting the next developments in a life that was beginning to have some sunshine in it at last.

Ellie and Joe depart after the wedding reception, their car covered in rice.

Joe finally had his orders for Ft. Leonard Wood, Missouri, so on September 9, 1942, I quit my job, packed Mother's big steamer trunk with my belongings and said goodbye to Cleveland. I boarded the train for what was to be our one-year-to-the-day together.

Ruth made one attempt to get me to either continue contributing to the apartment rent or move her to a hotel and put the furnishings in storage. But it didn't work. With Joe's support, I refused to be manipulated. I vetoed both those ideas and bade her adieu.

Glowing from my marriage to Joe and released from her, the apartment, and the traumas of the past few years, I boarded the train for St. Louis in elated anticipation of an exciting, though uncertain, future.

Chapter 7: Camp Follower

Army Habitats

Joe and Ellie begin a military life together.

September, 1942:

The first little flimsy house on the base of Ft. Leonard Wood was a far cry from anything to which I was accustomed, especially since it was furnished with army cots and orange crates. But autumn in the Ozarks was spectacular.

Soon we moved across the street to a place that at least had some real furniture in it. Such a tiny house on the post, but it brings to my mind the warmest kinds of memories. The buildings were all heated with coal in those days, and for years since, whenever I would smell coal smoke in the air, I would remember that beautiful autumn at Ft. Leonard Wood in the Ozarks.

I shopped for groceries at the PX and somehow learned to prepare meals from a little book called *Cooking for Two*. Just as did everyone in my generation, I read a lot, listened to the war news and music on the radio (Bing singing "White Christmas" comes to mind), and Joe and I held hands at every movie that was shown at the base theater.

In October, my suspicions were confirmed by a doctor at the base hospital that I was pregnant. For a while that day, I feared I might get into the wrong line and end up in Officer School! Joe and I were kind of overwhelmed with the idea—and excited! In November, Joe had a leave and we spread the good news to Ruth, Howard, and Alice in Cleveland and to the ecstatic Bainers in Meadville.

The war was going full blast in Africa, so in mid-November, the 6th Division was ordered to Arizona for desert maneuvers. With John Williams, a close friend of Joe's who was also originally from the 107th, and his Cleveland bride Liz, we left for Yuma in their 1940 Buick. We had Thanksgiving dinner in a restaurant in Tulsa, Oklahoma, each remembering family holidays of the past, but grateful for having each other this year.

There was scarcity of living quarters, especially for two couples, but finally we were taken in by Mr. and Mrs. W.O. Shipp who lived in a shabby little ranch house outside of Yuma. As their contribution to the war effort, they moved to the enclosed porch and gave us two bedrooms and a bath. The linoleum floors could be mighty cold when the temperature dropped to sixty degrees and there was no heat except the pot-bellied stove in the living room, but they were easy to sweep when the guys would arrive on Friday nights and stomp half the desert onto the floors.

We arranged for Liz and me to have our rooms and daily meals with the Shipps, and the guys would join us on Fridays for their weekend respite. Mrs. Shipp only knew about frying food but managed, somehow, using our combined meat and sugar ration books, to get three meals a day on the table. Liz and I knitted sweaters for the Red Cross, drank iced tea, played cribbage, read, and sunbathed outside during the week next to Mrs. Shipp's antique washer, which was kept under a kind of a shed in the yard.

We mostly acted as if it were summer instead of wintertime. We had a little Christmas tree that year and put the 6th Division insignia—a red star—on top of it. On weekends we sometimes went out to dinner or to the movies, but we were content to just sit around the ranch and eat Mrs. Shipp's cooking. Every Sunday, the Shipps' sons and their families would come and spend most of their day going through the irrigation procedure of their parents' land. Because the hired hands were away at war, one Saturday the four of us helped to herd a neighbor's sheep from one pasture to another, though I was getting a little large for climbing under wire fences. It was a long day, over and under. I thought Joe looked like Jesus as he carried the youngest of the lambs!

After General Montgomery's Desert Rat campaign defeated Rommels' Africa Corps, the 6th division was sent to Camp San Luis Obispo, California. We said goodbye to the Shipps, told the guys we'd see them there, and Liz and I took off in the Buick. We went by way of La Jolla where Liz had some friends. The traffic in Los Angeles was overwhelming; the town jammed with servicemen and women dressed in dark, city clothes while Liz and I were in blouses and skirts—mine quite tight.

Ellie and David (Dave), now a teenager, pose in 1959 in front of the San Luis Obispo house where he spent his first three months in 1943.

The four of us finally located a run-down cottage in Morro Bay on the coast of California—more linoleum floors but a "beach look" was added by a clam shell attached to an overhead light cord in the living

95

room. All the rooms were painted green. There were two bedrooms with a bath in between, a living room, and a small porch boarded by calla lilies that grew wild, and an antiquated kitchen where Liz and I combined forces to produce meals and where we played Cribbage by the hour. But there were calla lilies growing all around the porch and the guys were home every night for dinner, unless they were Officer of the Day.

Ellie holding David in a photo Joe carried to the
South Pacific.

I never did learn to Jitterbug. Either I was pregnant or busy with a new baby, but that's one dance craze that passed me by. No big deal! On June 18, 1943, we gave birth to David Calvin Bainer. I knew nothing about taking care of babies without someone telling me so these early days were quite an adventure amidst all the uncertainty of the war.

Joe, David, and Ellie before the farewells.

As I later described in a letter to David in 1990:

> *Early in the morning of June 18, 1943, I awoke with some very definite twinges. The hospital in San Luis Obispo being quite a ways away, Joe and I hurried to get me there. You weren't born until three o'clock in the afternoon and there wasn't a prouder father in the place. He informed me that you were the biggest baby in the nursery (you weighed 8 ½ pounds) and definitely the best looking. As we held you and inspected you—as new parents do—we were a little concerned about what felt like a soft lump on the top of your head, on the side. When we questioned Dr. Butler about it the next day, instead of his saying to such a naïve, worried couple "Not to worry—it will probably go away," he said, "If it doesn't improve in a week or*

so, we'll have to take him to University of Southern California Hospital–spinal meningitis, you know."

I stayed in the hospital ten days, dangling my feet out of bed on the eighth day which was custom, and each day we watched your beanie get smaller and smaller and felt more and more relieved. No wonder I was weak and woozy when I returned with you to the little cottage at Morro Bay.

When Joe wired Meadville, Momo and Popo and Mary were jumping for joy, especially since we had chosen my father's middle name, Calvin, for yours and Joe's dad's middle name for your first name. They sprinted out to look at another friend's newborn son, also named David, just to have an idea of what you might look like.

Fortunately the wife of one of the officers was a nurse, Mary Lou Behymer, who taught this poor, fumbling mother how to hold, bathe, and nurse you. After you were fed and settled in your plain bassinet with wheels, I'd do the washing by hand (in that same sink) and hang your little clothes and diapers on the line. Since Morro Bay is often fog shrouded, often I'd drag in the still-damp laundry late afternoons to be draped around the cottage all evening. The guys, meantime, would be sunburned and hot from the weather on the other side of the mountain at camp.

To weigh you, I would carry you to the local grocery store where I used the scales in the meat market. I nursed you on an exact four-hour schedule, but since you weren't gaining, the Doctor changed you to Similac, a powdered formula, and it was back to the kitchen for the tedious process of sterilizing all the utensils and bottles and concocting the formula.

You slept in a bassinet on wheels and were fed on a four-hour schedule, come what may. What a ridiculous way to care for an infant, but that's what the books said in those days. If you'd be howling in your bassinet, Joe would march in and order, "At ease!" You were a hungry baby and I waited too long to give you solid food, but I was completely inexperienced.

Joe loved looking at and holding his infant son, especially since we were getting suspicious feelings about the 6th Division

*departing. Instead, the Division was divided into two sections—
one that would leave in August for Texas and the other, to be
shipped out to Hawaii. John was appointed to the latter, but
Joe's orders were to go to Texas. He agonized over whether he
should accept them or apply for a transfer back to the troop
where he knew the men and they had trusted him as their
Lieutenant. I wanted no part of his decision. Finally, he did
ask to go with the Hawaiian detail, he was accepted, and as
Headquarters Troop, they were to leave a week before the rest
of the Division did.*

*We had such little time to get ready to say goodbye. I was
so upset I had to stop nursing you. Every morning we would
awaken in each other's arms, surrounded by an air of dread,
but the day finally came and with leaden hearts, we kissed
each other—and Joe kissed you—and he was gone.*

Chapter 8. The Long Road to Meadville

Ellie and David, 1943.

September, 1943:

After the wrenching farewells, Joe, John, and the rest of the Headquarters Team left for San Francisco where the division would all be shipped out at some mysterious date on some unknown ship. Liz and I packed up for our cross country trek, she to Cleveland, David and I to Meadville, where we were to spend the duration of the war with Joe's parents.

Today the very thought of the grueling trip across the country brings back the nightmare that it was. One option, briefly considered, was of my flying home with David, but there were lurid tales of civilians, with or without infants, being bumped from flights because the military took preference. Besides, Liz was three months pregnant and had to get the Buick back to her mother's home in Shaker Heights and I couldn't even consider her doing it alone, even though at the time I hadn't yet learned to drive. Also, she needed the additional gas ration cards issued to me and even David.

I mailed to Meadville everything but the absolute necessities for the trip, which included all the paraphernalia that traveling with a three-month-old baby involved. On a morning in September, 1943, with David in his bassinet in the back seat of the car, the white enamel "potty" with lid I had purchased to hold ice and formula-filled bottles on the floor behind the passenger seat, and suitcases in the trunk, we left Morro Bay and headed for our first stop—Oakland. Sometime after our second night spent in a cabin at Lake Tahoe, we picked up Rt. 66, which was the fastest route across the country in those days. Even in the open spaces of the West we had to obey the Victory Speed Limit of thirty-five miles per hour.

I did drive the Buick across the Great Salt Flats, eyes glued to the road, when the monotony would have made a practiced driver fall asleep at the wheel. In the desert, Liz and I would suck on the fast-melting ice in the improvised container—no such things as today's coolers then. Also, no laundromats. No pampers. I used some stiff, brown gauze-lined paper diapers on Dave until they ran out. It was a marvel he didn't become bow-legged from them.

I'd stop at remote little cafes to heat his bottle when his strict four-hour schedule called for it, and Liz and I would try to grab a bite at the time. David slept through the days from the motion of the car, but night time was exhausting.

West of the Mississippi, motels with kitchens were available, and when we'd stop, Liz and I would wheel in the bassinet. Then I would bathe and feed David, do some hand washing and pray it would be dry by morning, eat something, and go through the formula making ritual. After restless nights, we'd repeat the procedure until it all became a blur. In Denver we were held up with tire troubles—even retreads were a rare commodity during the war years. Of course, David slept through the whole, noisy tire changing procedure up on the hoist.

The drive across the prairie was long and tedious, and we began to run out of decent motels with kitchens, having to settle for crummy little cabins with newspaper stuffed in the holes in the wall. Then we lost our appetites, occasionally munching on a candy bar.

We had looked forward to Chicago, where arrangements had been made for us to stay in the apartment of Popo's sister, Aunt Betty, and her husband. In the middle of the six o'clock rush hour and with David howling at the top of his lungs to be fed, I called her from a pay station, only to learn that the guest room mattress had been "sent out to be cleaned (?)," but that there was a nice apartment hotel in their neighborhood where reservations had been made for us. After we finally located it, I snatched the still-crying David out of the bassinet, grabbed a bottle from the pot, and yelled at Liz that I wasn't dragging that basket into a hotel, as if it were her fault.

Having checked us in and finding our room on the 7th floor, she discovered David placidly nodding off to sleep in a drawer I'd yanked out of the dresser and filled with a pillow and placed him on top. I apologized for my outburst and we both started to laugh with a little hysteria thrown in.

We had been on the road nine days and nights from California with our husbands headed God knows where and for how long, and all we wanted was a drink or two and a quiet dinner, and to forget the baby and the war and the drive still ahead to Cleveland. So, I rejected Aunt Betty's telephone offer to stay with David, and Liz and I found a booth in the hotel dining room where we managed to eat some Chinese food and unwind for a few minutes. I did the formula number later in Aunt Betty's kitchen while Liz went to bed and we were both grateful that it was our last night on the road.

I'll never forget the expression on the face of Liz's mother as we drove into her driveway and she saw David wearing nothing but a diaper and a sweater over bare skin. I'd long since run out of clean clothes for the poor child and it took a few days for Liz's mother and her maid to get us back in shape again. When Liz saw her doctor about her pregnancy, he warned against her driving a car at this crucial three-month stage. He was flabbergasted at her announcement that she had just driven home from California. He would have keeled over if she had revealed the trip diet!

I stayed with Howard and Alice a week, showing David off and resting. Auntie "Lor" visited and said his face showed "good breeding." The Bainers could not wait for us to come to Meadville, and they drove over to see and hold their grandson. Momo said afterwards that her first impression was that though he was beautiful, he had such a thin little face. It must have matched mine because by then I was a wraith.

Before leaving Cleveland, I made an appointment for David to be checked by a recommended pediatrician in the Medical Building. Momo drove over to take us there and then return with us to Meadville. She parked the car in front of the building and accompanied us to the doctor's office. The doctor recommended Pablum and other solid food be added to David's regime and remarked to my delight, how skillfully I handled the baby, thanks to Mary Lou Behymer's teaching.

When Momo went for the car, she found it had been towed away, but when the police heard her tale of woe, they said, "OK, OK, we'll bring it to you and you just take it and your family back to Pennsylvania and stay there."

Chapter 9. Sunset

435 Sunset Drive, Meadville, Pennsylvania

435 Sunset Drive, Meadville, Pennsylvania (1942).

Fall, 1943:

As I look back, I realize that when I was introduced as Ellie Bainer in Meadville, Eleanor Hinig had become just a familiar but a shadowy figure, as if from some old movie—another person from another life. After the shabby environment of the recent past, moving into the Bainers' wallpapered pink guest room with a crib, a rocker, and a fireplace seemed like a luxury to me. However, after a week of hearing David's little baby noises in the night, I changed to the closet, dresser, and twin bed in Mimi's room, where I would remain.

David and I were warmly welcomed to the Bainer household which also included seven-year-old Nancy, and Justine, a kind of built-in maid who didn't last long after I came with a baby, but who would be replaced by a series of Allegheny College girls who "lived in." The household was definitely a busy one. The first week we were there, Momo entertained her Philo Club and Mimi promised me that when that was over, things would quiet down. In ensuing years, I would remind her of that unfulfilled promise.

Nancy was busy with school and Mimi with her job at the college; Popo with the bank and the Draft Board; and Momo, the "Old Ladies and Children's Home" Board, Monday afternoon Bridge Club, Philo, and Literary Club plus planning meals, buying groceries, cooking and washing every Monday with a wringer washer. I helped in whatever area I was needed.

No one was ever too busy to miss playing with David. He was the toy of the house, sometimes even being awakened at night to be passed around and cooed at. I remember Popo saying one morning that every household needed a six-month-old baby in it all the time.

Mimi and I became inseparable friends and through her I met her other friends. I was asked to join bridge groups and became a member of the City Hospital Auxiliary. When Janet and George DeArment and their baby son moved to North Main Street at the bottom of the Sunset Drive hill, people used to say they could set their clocks by Janet's and my walking by with her Jimmy and my David—first in buggies, later in Taylor Tots and sometimes on sleds.

Except for the daily V-Mail letters from Joe, the blue stars in windows indicating a serviceman lived there, and Popo's reports about the Draft Board, the war seemed very far away. Having lived on or near army posts, seeing so many young men in business suits and life appearing so normal was disconcerting. Sometimes I would go to Cleveland on the train, especially after Liz gave birth to her son in March, but I was always glad to return to Meadville, which felt like home.

Some memories I have of the war years: Meadville had a Civil Defense Corps and we had blackout curtains. For two years America went without weather reports, the government worrying the enemy would use them to plan bombing raids. Because nylon was going for parachutes, we wore wrinkly rayon stockings that plummeted to the floor the instant one's garters released them. In the summertime we wore leg makeup and mine always streaked. Food rationing meant each man, woman, and child in the country received a book of colored stamps to be given with payment for scarce foods like meat, oils, butter (4 oz. a week), cheese, and sugar. Later liquor was rationed, gasoline was doled out at three gallons a week, and shoes three pairs a year. Toilet paper was even scarce—"especially in that household of females," as Popo often complained. Everything had a use; grease was collected, for example, which provided glycerin for ammunition. There were scrap drives and Bond Rallies and children like Nancy bought war stamps. To my dismay, chocolate was hard to come by, as were tea and coffee, the latter of which I learned to drink in Meadville but with cream and sugar like Mother always did.

"David's Harem" is written on the back of this photograph from 1943. Mimi (left), Liz (center), and David and Ellie (right).

But mostly I remember how completely and wholeheartedly united Americans were in World War II. We read the newspapers avidly and followed the war on the radio or newsreels before the movies.

To lighten the mood at home, we read aloud books, such as those by Robert Benchley, and laughed uproariously. Mimi and I always had books at bedside—I still remember reading *Forever Amber* and some of those other wonderful ones we received monthly from Literary Guild Book Club. For outdoor fun, I would coast down Sunset Drive with Mimi and a neighborhood gang on snowy winter evenings. In the summer, David and I would enjoy the tiny beach at the Iroquois Club at Conneaut Lake. Sometimes when Nancy was not at school or playing with her best friend who lived up the street, she would plunk little David in her doll highchair and "teach" him arithmetic. She swears this is why he ended up an engineer when he grew up.

Photo of David, mailed to Joe, November 1943.
Caption states, "Probably looking for the bourbon."

Early on, Momo had taken me out on almost uninhabited Grandview Avenue and taught me how to drive. I took golf lessons from Jack Keillor at the Country Club, but never took the time to play.

I joined the Presbyterian Church and David was baptized one Sunday morning, with Momo praying on the corner for one more verse to the hymn as Popo and I were late in arriving with the "baptizee," but we made a photo finish entrance. It was in this church on June 6, 1944, where we joined throngs in prayer for the American, British, and Canadian troops as they stormed five separate Normandy Beaches—D-Day.

Chapter 10. How Can Emptiness Feel So Heavy?

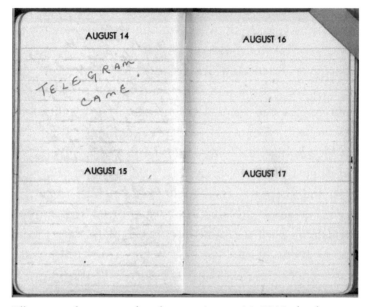

Ellie stopped writing in her diary on August 14, 1944, the day news about Joe's death arrived.

435 Sunset Drive, Meadville, Pennsylvania (Continued)

Though surrounded and welcomed by new family and friends, I was so often lonely and at loose ends. Where was Joe?

When we first parted—and David, Liz, and I made the long drive from California to Meadville—Joe went to Ranger School in Hawaii where he underwent additional training, which included a rigorous course on how to "Kill Or Be Killed." He stayed in Hawaii through December, 1943. We wrote V-Mail letters daily and planned for the future when someday the war would be over and he would work in a bank in Newark, Ohio. He already had contacted the President and had his enthusiastic endorsement of the idea. I think someday Joe might instead have come to Meadville to work at Merchants Bank with his father however.

After Joe was shipped out from Hawaii, we continued to write daily, though mail was often delayed on both ends, leaving me worried and wondering. We did receive some photos of Joe in "fatigues" marked "New Guinea: Feb-June, 1944," but it was hard for me to know where and when Joe went next because there was censorship. At one point, Liz's husband, John, wrote that he and Joe were together and *not* at the widely-publicized Battle of Saipan. I was so relieved!

We never learned which islands Joe had been on until his belongings were returned and we could read the names of the islands scratched on his mess kit. The Japanese were deeply entrenched in caves all along the chains of islands in the South Pacific and it was a tedious, bloody business both on land and at sea.

On August 12, 1944, Liz and baby Jeff came to stay with Mimi and me while the Bainers joined their friends, the Kirkpatricks, at their summer home at Gould Lake in Canada. I took the train to Cleveland and then drove back the same day to Meadville with Liz and her new baby—reminiscent of the past year's trip from California with baby David. We spent the next day just talking and taking care of babies. I wrote in my diary on August 13, "There are so many things I can say to Liz that I couldn't to anyone else, 'cept Joe—much shared about the past and about the present loneliness."

When the telegram came that Monday morning—August 14, 1944—I had just put David on the toidey seat in the powder room. I saw the boy on the bicycle and I *knew*. I did not have to read the words that Joe had been "KILLED IN ACTION."

Mimi was at work, and Liz and Jeff were still upstairs asleep. I never felt so alone in my life!

From that moment on I was in a state of dazed shock. Mechanically, I wandered upstairs and woke Liz whose immediate reaction was rage. I must have taken David off the seat, but I don't remember it. I called Mimi who, thoughtfully, stopped at the doctor's on the way home from work to get some kind of "calming" pills. My brother Howard was in the Finance Corps, stationed at Fort Benjamin Harrison, but I called Alice. She was devastated.

Together Mimi and I were able to reach the house in Canada next door to where Momo and Popo were staying. The people told Popo, but he simply told Momo that Joe had been injured and that they must go right home. She said he hummed all the way home and didn't talk, but she, too, *knew*.

People were in and out of the house. It was as if a bomb had hit Meadville.

After the official telegram was delivered, a strange thing happened. We had an uncensored letter from a Navy Captain who told us that part of his duty was to identify any military person who died on his ship. It was anchored off Hollandia, New Guinea, when a dying army officer was brought aboard. The Captain was Bob McFarland's brother and he knew immediately his body was that of his brother Bob's best friend, Joe Bainer. He described the ring he wore that I had given him and the personal effects in his wallet. One was a slip of paper on which the words "To thine own self be true" were printed. So, we knew it was Joe.

No longer did we cling to the hope that the wrong middle initial on the telegram had given us. Unlike some families who never were sure about their loved ones, we were now certain.

We all wept.

Joe's wallet, returned along with his belongings, still shows the calendar of last month he was alive ~ July, 1944.

A Memorial Service was held at the First Presbyterian Church in Meadville and the church overflowed. Finally the war had hit town. People were wonderful, but it's all kind of a blur. I had David, and the Bainers asked me if I would stay. It was touching how relieved they were that I was not going to take David away from them.

One of the hardest times I had was when Joe's foot locker was returned months later. Somehow it's always the little things that make the tears flow. In his travel shaving kit, down in the corner, was a little piece of soap that I had given Joe on Father's Day in California with the fading message still stuck to it: "Hi, Dad."

It hurt the first time I saw a soldier with the red star on his sleeve from the 6th Division. First holidays were hard: Thanksgiving, Christmas, New Year's Eve. But somehow after they were over, I felt as if another hurdle had passed and all I had to do was keep on getting past hurdles.

Another reason was that when I did start to weep, I felt a sickness that was hard to recover from. "How can emptiness feel so heavy?," I often wondered.

I had always thought that if anything happened to Joe, I would pack up David and go out West and start life over. I have always been grateful that I did not. I simply could not take the Bainers' grandson away from them, and they had become my family as well.

I cared for David. I ate, slept, and even laughed, but inside the emptiness still felt as heavy as stone. It would be a long time before I could react emotionally, and when the tears did come, they did not relieve the pain. I felt I must be strong for Joe's parents, as they didn't know what they would do if I fell apart—so sometimes I would quietly weep in the middle of the night or when I was in the shower.

PART IV. LEW (1944-1948)

Connections

In some mysterious
cosmic way
we are all
connected.

Is it our mutual
humanity...
destiny...
karma...
when souls meet souls
in what appears
to be
coincidence?

- Eleanor Hinig Davies

Chapter 11. Healing on Water

Ellie on a swing at Conesus Lake, New York, August, 1947.

Spring, 1945:

For something to do, I took piano lessons. I wasn't very good (and could only play "These Foolish Things"). I needed something more to look forward to, so I spent a lot of time thinking about David's and my upcoming summer at nearby Conneaut Lake. Through the kindness and generosity of Mr. and Mrs. Lowry Humes, we were to rent their three-bedroom cottage with the cathedral ceiling living room for a paltry $300 for the three-month season. They were moving next door to their huge summer home where their daughter, Jane, and granddaughter, Carol, would spend most of the summer as well, to be joined on weekends by Jane's husband, Ernie.

The Cottage at Conneaut Lake, Pennsylvania

The Red Wing ferry (right) at Conneaut Lake, Pennsylvania, with the infamous roll-down canopies that David called "Pop-Lo's," is shown in this postcard from the 1950s. Credit: Antique and Classic Boat Society.

Summer, 1945:

Just before his second birthday on June 18, David and I moved to the lake with all our belongings. I even had a truck cart the big sandbox from the Sunset Drive house to be placed outside the kitchen window where I could keep my eye on him.

Upon meeting my shy little son for the first time, Major Humes said, "I'm your pal" and henceforth we called him that. Pal and I used to laugh at the "terrible two-year-olds," Carol and David, vying over who was going to be at which end of the teeter-totter. They were together constantly—on the swings and in the sandbox and, afternoons, on the beach.

I had many visitors, including Ruth for a week, Auntie "Lor," Alice, and Howard (on leave from his post at Martinsburg, West Virginia). Jean Brown drove over for a day with some Sherwin-Williams friends. For most of July and August, Liz and Jeff lived with us, and possessive David spent most of his time making sure Jeff wasn't playing with one of his toys.

Our life had a very leisurely pace, except for the one day a week Liz and I and the boys would go to the Bainers in Meadville and do the washing, hang it on the lines to dry, shop for groceries, and go to the liquor store. We used to buy some awful unrationed whiskey which we would doctor enough to make a passable Old Fashioned. One night there was a B.Y.O.B. backyard party for all the Lake neighbors, to which Liz and I took this infamous product, placed it at the back of the table, drank the good stuff, and sneaked it home afterwards.

To David's delight, we would sometimes take the boat, the Red Wing, to Conneaut Lake Town for supplies. The boat had rolled up awnings which David called "Pop-Lo's" and he was a bit leery of them—no one knows why—especially since we had some rolled-up rugs in the Sunset Drive basement he called by the same name!

Mimi had started dating Bill DeArment so they used to come out evenings and Liz and I used to cluck knowingly as we watched the relationship blossom. Bill was the brother of George DeArment and together they ran the family tool business, now known as Channellock.

On August 6, 1944, an American B-29 bomber dropped the world's first atomic bomb on Hiroshima which signaled the end of the war—which for me had ended the summer before, not that I was not prayerfully thankful that it was over for everyone else at long last.

In late August, Captain LaPlace, Joe's former commanding officer, came from Illinois to pay his respects and sympathy to Joe's parents and me, and he told us the true story of Joe's death. We learned that Joe was killed on June 30, 1944, on the island of Millersburg opposite Hollandia in New Guinea where a huge invasion was going on. Their squadron was to neutralize the island and as their tanks rolled along inland from the shore and found no opposition, the tank lid was rolled back and Joe stuck his head out. Accidently, a gun being held by a soldier in the tank behind went off and the bullet pierced Joe's head. He was taken immediately to the beach and then by boat to the Navy vessel in the harbor and given intravenous transfusions en route. As we had already been told, Joe died on that ship, commanded—as fate would have it—by his best friend's brother.

I had a pressure headache for days. Gradually, I learned to accept what had actually happened, and that Joe's death had been a tragic accident.

David and I stayed until the middle of September, the nicest time at Conneaut Lake. It was during this quiet time that I decided I needed something more to look forward to.

The Digs at Daytona Beach, Florida

Daytona Beach Cottage, 1946.

January, 1946:

At the Lake, I formulated a plan in my mind that somehow David and I would go to Florida after the holidays. By the time January rolled around, Howard had been sent overseas for postwar duty and Alice was available and interested in joining David and me.

Through a friend of Auntie "Lor," we rented, sight unseen, an apartment in Daytona Beach for February, March, and April for the three of us. At the end of January, I sent the familiar steamer trunk via Railway Express to our address in Florida and met Alice on January 31 in Cleveland to stay overnight before our flight. Alice stayed with David while I met Rus Wardley, formerly of the "Club Residence," for dinner. How he'd changed! No longer the fun-loving and affable Rus, but instead a very subdued man whose eyes reflected the agony he had endured with the ill-fated 101st Airborne in the D-Day invasion. My heart was so heavy that night that I barely slept, so I straggled to the airport with David and Alice as her parents saw us off.

The engine prop airliner took seven long hours from Cleveland to Jacksonville during which time David was happily occupied with a pinwheel held next to the air vent. Poor Alice was deathly ill the entire trip so we gratefully spent a quiet night in a Jacksonville hotel before taking the train the next day to Daytona Beach. Long trip, which today takes three hours!

121

What a relief to finally arrive, and Alice and I were overjoyed when we saw our Daytona place—the lower floor of a white, two-story building on a quiet street within walking distance of the beach. David's front bedroom held a small single bed, with headboard painted royal blue to match the dresser and night table, and Alice and I shared a double bed in our room. The living room was comfortably furnished and the kitchen was all white tile. The very first week Alice and I made a pact: I'd clean the toilet if she'd kill the bugs.

We soon learned that just because it was Florida didn't mean it was warm, so while tow-headed little David played with a bucket and shovel, we languished in the sandy, protected back yard until well into March.

In the apartment upstairs lived a couple with two little girls; Fern was close to David's age so once again, he had a playmate. Their father was benefitting from the sun as he had been medically discharged from the Army with Ataprine poisoning—a yellow fever preventative drug which had caused all his body hair to fall out. We exchanged friendly conversation with them and occasionally had them in for drinks in exchange for emergency use of their phone, as we had none.

One such time was when I had to call a doctor to come to see David as he had a severe case of the flu. He gave him an injection of Penicillin—newly discovered then—and left vials and needles for me to give him injections every four hours. One of the most difficult things I ever did was to push that needle into the flesh of little David's bottom. I learned what it meant to say, "It hurts me more than it does you."

Alice was wonderfully supportive as she always has been my whole life.

After three months of sand and sunshine, David and I returned home, saying farewell to Alice, who would be joining Howard in Austria, and to Mimi, who was taking her eleven-year-old daughter and her bedroom furniture to her new life in an apartment on Spring Street. Bill DeArment started calling her "Meem"—and so did the rest of us after that.

In retrospect, I also realize how blessed I was all through those years of being a widow by having the warm, wonderful friendship of Alice, Mimi, Liz and Jean—deep friendships that became lifelong.

122

Mimi, now Meem, wrote me a very touching letter in April, 1946, asking me to be her attendant at their May 16 wedding in the living room of the Sunset Drive house. She kept reassuring me that even when she was wed, our friendship would remain as close as ever. I knew in my heart that it could not, but appreciated her saying it anyway.

To refurnish what was now *my* bedroom, I went to Cleveland where Ruth and I prowled through the storage warehouse and I selected a walnut bedroom set, a matching desk and chair, and Mother's chaise longue to be shipped to Meadville. I wish now I had included my oil painting, but I knew there was no place to store it at the Sunset Drive house. In the early days of the French House my father had purchased three huge oils—one for each of us. Howard's was a seascape, Ruth's was a colorful autumn scene, and mine was a Dutch family in their kitchen.

That day in the warehouse would be the last time I would be surrounded with all such tangible memories of home, including the buffet containing Mother's silver and cartons of her gold-edged china. So much had happened in the five years since the "Club Residence." Ruth would later marry some man she met in a bar at the Hotel Carter, move to Columbus, and, not having paid the charges, all of the goods would be sold at auction. She never told me or perhaps I would have rescued them—although I don't know with what money! I know they were just "things" but they were Mother's and I felt a sense of loss when Ruth told me long after it had been a *fait accompli*.

After my bedroom was settled, it was time to move David from the little back bedroom to which his crib had been relocated from the pink guest room when he was about nine months old. Momo and I took great pleasure in fixing up what was Nancy's former bedroom to be his. I painted the headboard of a small bed white along with a chest of drawers, shelves for toys, and a wicker chair while Momo made the cushion for it and a bedspread of red wide wale corduroy. It was the beginning of deep and lasting relationship between the two of us.

Momo became a combination of a mother, friend, and confidante. What a privilege for me to have been close to Otelia Fox Bainer, who was beloved and revered by everyone who ever knew her; a loving compassionate Christian lady whose abiding faith was lightened by a sense of humor and fun—and she was a great cook! Joe had told Momo before she met me that he found a girl who reminded him of her. That's the best compliment I've ever received, but I surely fell short on the cooking part!

Momo and Ellie hang laundry at 435 Sunset Drive.

She and Popo were one of the most devoted couples I've ever known. Except to his wife, he was not a man who could express love easily, but I'll never forget the interest he took in me. He was the first older man I had known who really listened to me and was always very supportive of me when I needed him most. His successful battle with colon cancer was fought with courage and incredible patience and he encouraged others with the disease to be courageous as well.

After Meem was married, Momo told me one day as we were folding laundry that she and Popo wanted me to know before I ever met anyone that they hoped I'd marry again. In my heart I wondered if I'd ever find the right man someday.

Chapter 12. Sparks Flying

435 Sunset Drive, Meadville, Pennsylvania (Continued)

June, 1946:

One rainy day during the summer of 1946, as I was waiting with David in the car at the railway station for the 11 a.m. freight train to roar past (a frequent delight for him), I realized that the time had come for me to develop new friendships and activities of my own. That summer I had played a little golf and, in the fall, I joined the newly formed Ping Pong league.

I knew I must fill the void that Meem's leaving had created. Therefore, it was with delight that I accepted an invitation to attend a luncheon at the Meadville Country Club where I quickly became friends with Edna Turner and Kay Frisk. I was asked to join a bridge club and expanded my friendship with Margie Moore and "Mame" Gamble, each of whom had a delightful sense of humor. We would all be friends for life, in fact, as it turned out.

When I visited Betty Lamprecht Slobey and Buck at their apartment in East Orange, New Jersey, we shopped in New York and, for the first (and only) time in my life, I bought a pair of high-heeled shoes. Janet and George DeArment were always kind enough to drag me places along with them as a third wheel and George remarked to me when I returned wearing spike heels that "You don't look *that* much different," but his head was tilted way back.

Meem had developed different friends in a crowd from the Country Club, among whom was Mary Lou Walker. When she and her husband Lew returned from his stint in the Navy, he became head of Talon, Inc.—a zipper company founded by his grandfather.

Meadville was Lew Walker's town, so important was Talon to its economy. Several thousand people worked for the company, and it stayed robust even during the Depression. So it was a surprise to meet his brother, Bob, who really didn't seem to care a hoot about the place to which I had become so attached. He spent some time in town after

127

the Navy and we started to date. At the time he was still stinging over his wife, Edie, who divorced him without giving any reason, according to him. He spent a lot of time questioning Edie's actions and talking a lot about himself.

However, Bob was slender, nice looking, and soft-spoken, and I was flattered by the attention from this local millionaire. At first it was exciting and different to be dating again, but I began to resent his trying to "educate" me in his Princeton ways. He also intimated that should we ever become serious enough to marry, David would be relegated to a nursery. Not the right guy for me, I thought.

This was my situation in February, 1947, when Bill Williams called and asked if I would go to the Charity Ball with his ex-Coast Guard buddy nicknamed "Giesel" after a character in the *Popeye* comic strip. Bill and his wife, Jeannette, had become good friends and so, although I had met this raucous and somewhat homely guy in Cleveland, I accepted.

Meanwhile, over coffee every morning at Wirt's Drug Store, Bill Williams, who had an insurance agency, had become friendly with former Navy officer and 1940 Allegheny College graduate, Lew Davies, who was working for Warren Smith, one of Meadville's major automobile dealers. Lew accepted Bill's invitation to accompany his sister-in-law Mickey, who lived out of town, to the Charity Ball.

When Momo learned from Meem that there would be a group attending the dance, she planned a pre-dance party, inviting several couples. I remember standing in the hall, looking into the living room with Meem and Momo, and all three of us remarking how impressive was this brown-eyed, dark-haired and vitally attractive new man in town. Meem always maintained that when she asked Bill Williams where he'd found him, Bill replied, "Oh, I just save him for sisters-in-law," and she claimed she retorted, "Well, I've got a sister-in-law you can save him for."

Here's another remarkable coincidence: Jim Nichols was a close friend and a Phi Gam fraternity brother of Lew's from Allegheny College. He also lived at the "Club Residence." From those days, I also knew his wife, another Eleanor. Jim claimed that he introduced Lew to me at a Country Club reception during the Allegheny College commencement the June before and it didn't "take." Well, it "took" in February.

When Lew and I danced at the Charity Ball, sparks flew.

I still recall the thrill of Lew's first phone call to me the following week after Giesel had returned to Cleveland and Mickey to New Jersey. Readily I accepted his dinner invitation for the following Saturday night and counted the hours until the evening arrived. Remembering our first date at Wallers Restaurant brings to mind how sexy a voice I thought he had, the way he cradled his chin in his hand when he talked, and how secure I felt when he held me as we danced. When he brought me home, and we were sitting and talking in the living room, three-and-a-half-year-old David padded downstairs in his nightie-nights and climbed onto his lap. The affection Lew showed David at that moment crowned our evening together and I knew I had found the right man.

Several smooches later, our romance began. We dated all through snowy March and rainy April and he sent me Camellias for an Easter corsage. He spent the holiday with his folks in Sharon, however, as he had promised his younger sister Ruth that he would be there for their tradition of coloring eggs on Easter eve—demonstrating to me his love for family. Lew's father's history of strokes was the reason Ruth was in Sharon, as she'd promised her brother she would be there for her parents while he was in the Navy, and his other sister was married.

Lew's closeness to his Dad had influenced his decision to return to Meadville after the war instead of to Rochester, where he had worked at Liberty Mutual after graduating from Allegheny. His years in college had been crowded with jobs that ranged from waiting on tables to selling Fuller Brushes. Junior year, having convinced Dr. Tolley, the President, that he would be able to handle all the college publications at a profit, Lew spent a huge amount of time selling ads to the downtown merchants and became particularly well acquainted with them, especially Warren Smith.

Lieutenant Commander Davies, fresh from having spent four years of his life in the Navy, found he had to abandon his earlier ambition to become a corporate attorney. Allegheny College wanted to hire him, but the only salary the college could afford was too low for ambitious

Lew. So, Lew and Warren Smith came to an agreement that he would oversee Warren's tire operation until such a time that post-war Cadillacs and Oldsmobiles became readily available, when Lew would be General Manager of the entire agency.

Lew and Ellie on their first anniversary, in 1949.

I had written Bob Walker, who was then at Yale Law School, and told him about Lew and me and his response was rather sarcastic about this guy with his common Welsh name. Momo commented that it was a blessing that I was comparing Lew to Bob Walker, instead of to Joe!

When Bob was in town briefly in June, he called and casually suggested that I ride over to the Cleveland Airport with him, drop him off, visit my friends, and then drive his brand-new Buick convertible back to Meadville for him. Thinking of the appeal of driving that glamorous vehicle, I accepted; however, when I mentioned it to Lew, I sensed his negative reaction to the idea. I told Momo, "There's steel behind those brown velvet eyes." When he learned that I had called Bob back and declined his offer, it was a turning point in our relationship.

The rest of that summer of 1947, Lew and I went to some parties with friends, but mostly spent our dates together, getting to know each other and falling in love. We shared a lot in common and found that we mutually admired and liked each other. I learned that Lew had broken up with a singer in Philadelphia before we met, and I was glad about the timing. Her picture was still on the mantel one time when David and I visited Lew's apartment one day. I whispered to David to "hide" the picture, and Lew never found it again. Actually it was kind of a petty thing for me to do. Jealous streak?

Lew and Ellie in Conesus Lake, New York, August, 1947.

In August, 1947, Lew was invited to join two Rochester couples at a cottage they had rented at Conesus Lake in New York State and he arranged for me to take the New York Central from Erie to Rochester and to the lake for the weekend. We had such fun with Henry Shute and Janet, with whose mother Lew had boarded during the Liberty Mutual years. Janet had been a faithful letter writer to Lew all through his four years in the Navy. She was one wonderful and funny person, always a surprise to her more conservative husband. Tom and Marion Gaffney were also congenial and told me afterwards that when the skinny person that was me finally left to go swimming with Lew, everyone else cheered: "Now we can let our stomachs out."

When Lew asked me to marry him, the two of us were sitting at a little table at a lakeside restaurant with "Peg O' My Heart" playing in the background. Happily, I said "YES." After we returned and Lew made the announcement to the others, the two couples took off and came back laden with flowers and candles and champagne and we were feted at dinner and all evening.

We didn't become officially engaged until Labor Day Weekend, however. We were visiting our mutual friends, Jim and Eleanor Nichols, who lived in Bay Village, Ohio, a suburb of Cleveland. Because Lew and I had known the Nichols (separately) for years, it was a perfect setting for what was to happen. Their two children, Barbara and Scott, and my David were ramming around the Nichols' small house on Canterbury Road when quietly Lew steered me to the upstairs bathroom where he lovingly proposed and slipped a precious diamond ring on my finger. (His later version of saying, "Sit down, I want to talk to you," is total fabrication.)

To celebrate, the sparkling burgundy flowed and the bride-to-be had to be walked around the block before dinner. Actually, I hadn't been feeling very well for several weeks. I felt so tired all the time and had a nagging cough I couldn't seem to shake.

A visit to Howard and Alice's apartment, September 1947, to announce their engagement. The oil painting Howard was given as a child is shown in the background.

We stopped at Howard and Alice's to share our good news before leaving Cleveland and I wondered if I would ever make it home. Momo, having met us at the door that night, announced to Popo that "Ellie has ice on her finger, but a terrible cough." Sleepily, he questioned why I'd have ice on if I had a cold!

As the cough persisted, my doctor in Meadville, Dr. Muckinhoupt, admitted me to City Hospital where I received a series of heat treatments and medication. At first he brushed off the fact that there was a history of tuberculosis in the family, but X-Rays disclosed a very suspicious area in the upper lobe of my left lung. The specialist in Erie, Dr. Anderson, was attending a medical meeting out of town, so while awaiting his return, Dr. Muckinhoupt prescribed bed rest—not an easy assignment with a four-year-old who needed me.

The Bainers had planned to attend the annual Pennsylvania Bankers Association meeting in Atlantic City, so Momo asked Alice to come from Cleveland to stay with David and me. It meant she had to cook for us and sterilize my eating utensils, but Alice being Alice, she came graciously. Years later she confessed she had previously had tuberculosis peritonitis which had prevented her from ever bearing a child, and yet she took this risk on my account.

After the Bainers returned and Alice departed, Lew made arrangements for me to meet his family, even when it meant a bedside introduction. So, up the stairs one September Sunday afternoon trooped the Davies from Sharon. Although ill, Lew's father was a distinguished looking man with a crown of thick white hair. Lew's mother was a stout, peppy lady with a twinkle in her eyes and we were drawn to each other from the start. Also, I felt a warm rapport with his sister, Ruth, and her fiancé Daun Nesbit, as well as with his other sister, Helen, and her husband, Harry Locke. Helen and I long giggled over the fact that the first time we met she was wearing slippers as in her haste to leave home, she hadn't changed back into shoes.

Little Jimmy Lew Locke, Helen and Harry's son, was younger than David, but they played together happily during the visit. If it was disconcerting for them to meet Llewellyn's future wife lying down and ailing, no one showed it. The thought went through my mind that they had no idea how tall I was when I "stood up on end!" Of course,

Momo made a little party out of the occasion and it turned into a delightful, unforgettable afternoon.

Lew and Momo took me to see Dr. Anderson in late September, 1947. I remember hearing the World's Series on the radio in the car. Tuberculosis was his diagnosis and he recommended my going to a sanitarium. I felt as if a bombshell had been dropped in our midst. With calm practicality, he said I had a choice of either going to Cresson, a state institution where months of bed rest would be the treatment, or to the Newton Memorial Hospital in Cassadaga, New York, which was doing experimental work with a new antibiotic, Streptomycin.

Immediately we chose the latter and couldn't hide our disappointment when Dr. Anderson was told on the phone that there were no vacancies there.

I learned the next day about Lew's determination and persistence. He drove to Cassadaga, where he strode in the door of Newton Memorial Hospital and talked his way into seeing Dr. Rathbun, who was the head of the hospital. During the conversation, Lew learned that the doctor was an avid fisherman so he encouraged him to tell him all about his experiences. Lew told me that after about half an hour of this, Dr. Rathbun said, "You know, we *do* have a room," and before Lew left, the doctor arranged for me to come the very next day and stay in a former little examining room at the end of the Women's Floor in the Infirmary Building.

Lew and Momo agreed to drive me there and before I knew what was happening, I was packing my suitcase and calling to say goodbye to my friends. I promised Meem I would stop by their apartment, and with a handkerchief over my mouth to check out her baby son, William, born September 20, 1947, and already nicknamed "Buz" from Buz Sawyer in the comics. When Meem said farewell to me she told me she agreed with Jeannette Williams who had remarked, "What more can happen to that girl?"

The hardest thing I had to do was to say goodbye to my beloved David, especially when I didn't know for how long. I could barely stand it that I wasn't going to be the one to feed him, read to him, share his little jokes, and take his little hand in mine, walk to the playground or drive him to the railroad station to see the mighty freight train. In spite of my agony, I felt fortunate he would have the continuity of life with his loving grandparents who never indicated in any way that their independence was being threatened.

It was a quiet trip for all of us, each adrift in private thoughts. Momo told me later that going to Cassadaga in the car with Lew, she noticed my face was so thin she could see my teeth outlined against my cheeks. I was 5'11" and weighed just 130 pounds.

The austere hospital buildings were located at the end of a long, winding drive at the top of the hill which overlooked Cassadaga Lake.

Chapter 13. Cure Hour

Newton Memorial Hospital, Cassadaga, New York

In robe and slippers, Ellie poses in front of the Women's Building of
Newton Memorial Hospital.

October, 1947:

On the bed stand next to me was a sputum cup and a glass
thermometer in its alcohol bath. At the foot of the bed was a nunnery
dresser flanked by a chair—sparse furniture in a green-walled room. Just

yesterday, I had a dressing table, chaise, soft pillows. The only warmth came from the October sun that shone through a glass wall to a porch.

But, I was lucky to get a room here!

Other sanitariums of the day offered the long-traditional bed rest and fresh air and (not unusual) death. In this small sanitarium in Chautauqua County in Western New York, a young Chinese doctor was trying experimental doses of the antibiotic, Streptomycin, in syringes of hope.

As I lay in that narrow hospital bed, I wasn't thinking about how lucky I was that Lew had been able to wangle this little room for me. In this, one of my darkest hours, I was thinking: What in the world am I doing *here*? I should be at home with my little boy, making happy plans for a wedding to that wonderful man. We've been talking about a February date and a honeymoon in New Orleans. *And now this!*

"Cure Hour is over," announced a bustling nurse as she opened the door of my room in the infirmary. When I had been admitted an hour before, all had been quiet on the floor. But now how you could hear it: the coughing.

December 5, 2003:
Pulmonary Research Day, The Cleveland Clinic

When Dr. Mani Kavuru asked me to relate my experience in a TB Sanitarium, he had no way of knowing that my father had also undergone treatment for tuberculosis years before. Saranac Lake, America's first TB sanitarium, had achieved a widespread reputation for a successful cure by 1912, when my father must have met the two standards of admission of the founder, Dr. E. L. Trudeau: curability of the disease and financial resources. There he must have followed the Doctor's philosophy of healing the whole person, including fresh air and rest in healthful surroundings as well as developing an optimistic attitude. Prior to Trudeau, tuberculosis was considered a death sentence. At Saranac Lake, he offered hope for a possible cure. To his referring *physicians, he always stressed the importance of early detection for this contagious disease.*

But can you imagine making a lung disease diagnosis without X-rays? Dr. Trudeau challenged referring physicians to watch for lassitude, slight loss of appetite and weight, some coughing, and temperatures in the 99.5 to 100 degrees at irregular intervals. No wonder so many victims died when the insidious early symptoms could be so easily overlooked and diagnostic labs were rare.

Grace and Ruth Hinig visit Ben Hinig (right) at
the Trudeau TB Sanitarium in Saranac Lake
where he was a patient (c 1912).

All I have of my father's experience at Saranac Lake is the picture above, taken in front of one of the sanitarium buildings, showing my mother, my sister Ruth, and my father swathed in fur coats. Mother and Ruth must have gone by train from Cleveland to Saranac Lake, but visitors to patients could not stay longer than a week at this $1.00 a day "health *resort." I hope they found delight in the offered sleigh—bundled up in furs and blankets, warm bricks at their feet, gliding along the white expanses in exhilarating cold air!*

As a little girl, I remember my father taking a series of deep breaths of fresh air from his bedroom window every morning of every season. Every morning he had a raw egg from a shot glass. His snowshoes hung in a spare room closet, and he had an abiding interest in the Cleveland Fresh Air Camp and served on its board for many years.

I do not know how long he was at Saranac Lake. Upon discharge, patients were termed "apparently cured" once they had maintained a normal lifestyle for two years without relapse.

It never occurred to me that someday my TB experience would be of interest to anyone—much less a distinguished group such as yours.

When I had arrived earlier that day at Newton Memorial Hospital, I had no idea that I was in for a life-changing experience. I filled out the necessary forms in the Admittance Office while the October World Series of 1947 blazed from the radio. I learned that I wasn't going to be seen by my doctor, Dr. Timothy C.H. Liang, until he returned from California in a week or so. I was told I could walk about the halls and meet people except when the meal trays were delivered, or afterwards, when an hour of bedrest, called "Cure Hour," was required.

After breakfast and supper we were permitted to read, but after lunch for two hours we were supposed to sleep or at least lie still. Not having taken a nap since childhood, I spent that time doing a lot of thinking.

I was told I had tuberculosis, but if I *didn't* have it, I sure was going to get it here!

So, I was careful about exposure to the other patients, except for one splendid and classy woman named Janet Livermore who had a private room at the other end of the hall. Janet had tuberculosis of the spine. I always thought it was just a lung disease, but I learned it could attack any part of the body. Janet's exemplary courage and sense of humor jolted me out of my doldrums. I visited her frequently and we developed an immediate and strong bond. Janet was so special that in later years when I was pregnant, Lew and I thought that if we ever had a girl, we would name her "Janet," which also covered our two other Janets: Shute and DeArment.

My spirits were uplifted by heartwarming letters from Lew and his Sunday visits. He never showed the least temerity about exposure to the disease. I wasn't allowed to kiss him, but we would hold hands and his very presence was strengthening. He'd tell me about going up to the house to see David and read to him. Lew made me laugh when he told me of one evening when he was reading one of David's favorite books about a train that released itself from its tracks, and shouted, "I'm free, I'm free" to which David interjected, "I'm four!"

From this gloomy and depressing atmosphere, I was relieved to be called for my in-depth interview with Dr. Liang, the brilliant, discerning doctor who offered patients a supplemental treatment to bed rest. Since 1946, Dr. Liang had been advocating the use of Streptomycin in smaller doses and building them up in the course of treatment. Prior to him, doctors had administered such large amounts that the patient suffered severe side-effects. Although I was awed by this doctor who had cut in half the death rate from tuberculosis in Chautauqua County using his Streptomycin formula, I found him very approachable.

Dr. Liang had examined my X-Rays and in spite of his confirmation of the diagnosis, I felt better. He asked me a lot of questions about myself, and after I gave a recital of the sad events of the last ten years of my life, he pondered for a while and then simply stated that my body had reacted with the weakness to a disease my father had. "TB isn't inherited, but the tendency is," he said.

I guess I never took time out to grieve, I told the doctor. I always felt that I had to be strong for everyone else. "Unexpressed grief is not good," he quietly replied. "For years you have stuffed things inside—too much, too long. Now while your body heals here, you can let them out and let them go."

Then he brightened as he explained how successful his Streptomycin therapy was proving to be. He said that I would receive

500 mg by injection each day for a week and, as my tolerance built, 2 grams (2000 mg) a day for as long it takes. "You'll have that wedding yet, I guarantee," he told me. If I didn't experience the initial side effect of dizziness, I would be "promoted" to the first floor of the Women's Building. I decided right then that I would not be dizzy—and I wasn't.

DR. TIMOTHY C. H. LIANG HOLDS A VIAL OF STREPTOMYCIN USED IN HIS TB TREATMENT

Dr. Timothy C.H. Liang, Ellie's doctor, who had developed a new and more effective treatment for tuberculosis with smaller doses of Streptomycin.

The first time a nurse came in with that huge syringe, I looked around for the horse. I opted to have the injection in my rear end rather than in my thin arms, and by the end of the week, I had a very black bottom.

During those first weeks behind the closed door in that little room, I did a lot of reminiscing and crying. I wept for Daddy and with regret that we hadn't been closer. I wept for Mother, who also had stuffed *her* tears inside, and perhaps her body had paid for it with her life. And finally, I wept for Joe and the future of which he was robbed;

for Momo and Popo who had lost their only son; even for Meem who had lost a brother; and at last the tears freely flowed for myself and the sorrows of the past. I think that this release was every bit as therapeutic as was the medication, if not more so, because afterwards I was filled with a rush of gratitude: for Dr. Liang and his timely work with the new drug; for Momo and Popo taking adoring care of David in my absence; and mostly for Lew Davies and all he meant in my life—now and in the future that was looking brighter by the moment.

When no side effects to "Strep" were determined and a vacancy occurred, this new woman was moved to the Women's Building, with a stronger resolve than ever to get well.

The whole atmosphere of the Women's Building was more cheerful than the infirmary. The rooms contained two hospital beds, two dressers, and a closet and opened out onto a porch which was not often used, as autumn winds southeast of Buffalo bordered on the chilly. Every night, however, even throughout the long, cold winter, those porch doors were opened wide, regardless of the temperature. Shades of old pictures of my father bundled into a fur coat and covered with a robe at Saranac Lake in 1912, I thought. Actually it snowed in early November on that hilltop and the ground was not seen again until May!

I had a very quiet woman, named Martha, for a roommate, and she and I spent all of our time in pajamas and robes, but we were allowed with the other women on the first floor to walk to meals in the dining room a few rooms away. I used to go step on the scales after breakfast every morning, noting with glee every ounce I gained. We had a choice of taking Cod Liver Oil by capsule or the more effective (but foul-tasting) liquid, and I chose the latter. Every morning each of us would receive our daily shot of Streptomycin.

We were a strange mix of women, including a European war bride who had entered the same time as I and who was equally as eager to recover and get on with her life. There were whiners and encouragers just as in the outside world from which we were isolated. I heard a lot of poor grammar and obscene expressions. I was determined to be friendly, but not to sound as vulgar as they.

When the results of my sputum tests came up negative, Lew brought David up to see me. I was overjoyed to see him again, even if he spent most of his visit cranking my bed up and down. I had twinges when I saw how he had grown since I'd been away, but I certainly was joyful to witness the compatibility between Lew and my son. I was touched when he told me all about their having gone together to the Halloween Parade. The next day I was asked if I would be willing to lead a Sunday School class for the Women's Building patients, and with my faith in God gradually returning, I accepted, and I found it a restoring experience. I'd go visit Janet in the infirmary and thank God I was no longer there.

Ellie's painting from Occupational Therapy at the sanitarium
(1948).

One afternoon a week we would have Occupational Therapy and I tried my hand at oil painting. One—of a brown bowl and a lemon—was even worthy of framing. I spent hours lying with my left hand on my bedroom wall while the gleam of my engagement ring sparkled into long daydreams about my future.

I read a little and wrote a few letters. Bill DeArment kindly sent me daily postcards, and Bill Williams wrote me many hilariously funny letters. I saved his first letter, which vividly described his wild "night on the town" with Bill DeArment to celebrate the birth of Buz. While they patronized some of Meadville's less noble establishments, Bill Williams reassured me that Lew, "the tired tire-man is a paragon of clean living these days and won't even accept a bottle of beer...I have ordered a case of brass polish for his ever apparent halo."

Finally, the word came that I could move to the second floor—a big step in the direction towards home. Now I was allowed to get dressed and walk the short distance to the main Dining Room Building and only had to be in pajamas for afternoon Cure Hour and at night. Better still, I could go out with Lew when he came to visit on Sunday afternoons and could have other company too, including the steadfast Jean Brown and Howard and Alice from Cleveland. But mostly, Lew and I would have our Sunday afternoon dates—a chance to talk as we rode around the countryside and by the beaches of Lake Erie and then have leisurely dinners at the White Inn in Fredonia, New York. Every Sunday night I would reluctantly return, though tired, and every Friday, I would start grooming myself in anticipation of Sunday again.

I had an obnoxious roommate named Doris and one day I walked into our room and caught her reading my diary. She was divorced and man-crazy and made eyes at Lew, not knowing how amused he was when he saw her lying down with her falsies standing straight up.

With the song, "I'll Be Home For Christmas" playing on the radio, I became so excited at the prospect of going home for a week, I ran a low-grade temperature. Dr. Liang, in his understanding way, gave me permission anyway, and I'll never forget that Christmas in Meadville. Lew came for me and, back home, I felt a holiday glow being with David, Momo, and Popo who gave me a Bible as a Christmas gift. My own bed felt so good and the food was heavenly.

One night we went to the Country Club, where I ran into Bob Walker who told me I looked better sick than when I was well (the ten pounds I'd already gained apparently were becoming). I did notice that I tired easily, having missed my quieter "Cure Hours" because of the excitement of being home. A visiting nurse came in daily and administered my injection of Streptomycin, but on Christmas and New Year's, Momo gave them to me. During one injection, when David was

145

standing behind her with a balloon, I thought she and I would both go through the ceiling when upon withdrawing the needle, it exploded the balloon. New rule: no balloons in rooms with needles!

Ellie rests at Sunset Drive on a home visit while she was being treated. "TB Special" is written on the back.

Reluctant as I was to return to Cassadaga, I knew in my heart I wasn't ready for the "real world" yet. At the end of January, I would get my four months evaluation at which point a decision would be made on how long I needed to stay. So, the war bride and I were taken to Buffalo General Hospital where they had an X-Ray machine that showed deeper levels of the lung. The report showed that she could stop taking Strep and would be released a month later, but I would face two more months of Streptomycin shots followed by an undetermined sanitarium stay. The good news: I did not require pneumothorax.

Many of my fellow patients had "pneumo" and dreaded the huge (in their words) needle that forced air into the chest cavity to rest the diseased lung. Refills of two to seven liters of additional air were given every ten to fourteen days. How they hated it!

One patient I knew, a former nurse named "Red," underwent a drastic thoracoplasty. She returned to the infirmary where she endured extreme pain from the removal of ribs on the left side of her chest to permanently collapse the lung.

Unbelievably, in March, a shop opened in the basement of the Women's Building where cigarettes were sold. It didn't take long for most of us from the second floor to resume our long-forfeited pleasure. Today it seems appalling that smoking was allowed among patients trying to recover from lung disease! Of course, nothing was known then of the lethal effects of smoking on the lungs. When Lew paid me an unexpected visit, and found me puffing away, he was horrified. When I rationalized that cigarettes "won't hurt me," he retorted that they "sure won't do you any good either." I vowed to cut down but it was easy to be hooked.

Ellie, "after."

By mid-April, occasionally the weather permitted us to push our beds onto the porch for afternoon Cure Hours and *I was off Strep!* X-rays showed scar tissue had formed in my upper right lobe and Dr. Liang said the cannular shadows were gone; my TB was considered "arrested." I had gained 30 pounds and Lew said I had "calves and things." One by one I watched as my companions were discharged until finally it was my turn!

My joy was short-lived when I learned that as a Chinese National, Dr. Liang had been threatened with deportation as an alien on a student visa. However, to continue his beneficial research with Streptomycin, a bill was quickly passed by Congress, allowing him to be a permanent resident of the United States. The New York Times even reported the story on May 25, 1948, stating that Congress had granted Dr. Liang citizenship status because of the "almost miraculous" results of his "Cassadaga Formula" to treat tuberculosis at Newton Memorial Hospital. Amen to that.

When the day of my release finally arrived, I gave Dr. Liang a huge hug and promised I'd be back for regular six week check-ups. I said goodbye to "Red," other acquaintances in the infirmary (some had sadly died), and I watched Janet walk!

I will always be grateful for the blessing of having been in a place where, in the midst of old-fashioned Trudeau programs and settings, a visionary doctor was on the cutting edge of a cure for TB—a cure that would soon render sanitariums like Cassadaga obsolete. I was not only cured, but now I weighed 154 pounds and each pound I gained had brought me closer to home, family, and friends. Everything shone with a new future.

I realized that I'd had a spiritual, emotional, and psychological healing to accompany the physical one within those sanitarium walls.

On the sunny Saturday morning of May 15, 1948, Meem came for me in her convertible, and I practically skipped to the parking lot. Meem remarked how pretty Cassadaga Lake was and, for the first time, I observed the lake glistening below in the spring sunshine and realized that there had been hidden beauty amidst the ugliness all along.

In my haste to depart, I left all my clothes in the closet and they had to be mailed to me. I needed new ones anyway, in a larger size, and with longer skirts because the New Look had arrived. I had a New Look and surely a new outlook.

Home! I cannot describe the joy of being a mommy again and planning a wedding with my dear Lew who had driven in all weather conditions on twisty country roads to see me every Sunday of my eight-month stay.

I was at the turning point in my life.

My first twenty-eight years had been like a soap opera, and I was about to enter a life that was more like a fairytale. Lew and I were to be married in July and live happily ever after.

" I have a book."

–Eleanor's first sentence as recorded in her Baby Book, July 10, 1921.

Afterword

After the title page in her original memoirs, Ellie inserted a quote from Shakespeare, "The past is prologue." Life's hard lessons, once absorbed by a thoughtful twenty-eight-year-old, shaped the mother that I knew. The events of 1919 to 1948 were indeed the prologue for the rest of her life, and difficult as they often were, the tragedies did not define her, but rather helped shape her attitudes towards life, family, and the people and town she loved.

Ellie's story did not end in 1948, of course, but continued for another 70 years. She chronicled her first fifty years in her memoir, from which most of this book was excerpted. Perhaps one day we'll tell more of her story, although in many ways her poetry has eloquently done much of this work already.

Ellie and Lew's wedding day, 1948.

Ellie and Lew were married on July 27, 1948, in a ceremony in the living room of 435 Sunset Drive, the home of Momo and Popo Bainer. The announcements for the wedding, sent afterwards, referred to Eleanor Bainer as "their daughter." And she was. Momo and Popo became surrogate grandparents to two more boys who were born to Ellie and Lew in 1950 and 1951, Jack and Steve, and Meem and Unc (her husband Bill) were family to us too.

There is an expression that friends are the family you choose. This is a family Ellie chose for us all—rather than moving out West to start out fresh, surely a reasonable option for someone who had been through everything she had.

Our father, Lew, also chose David, or Dave as he became better known, as well as Ellie. He was part of a package deal, as Lew might have explained in the terms of the successful automobile dealer that he became only a few years later. When Lew and Ellie were married, he had spent four years in the Navy, and wanted to have a family. He always said he would be married before he was 30 and he beat that deadline by one week. Two for one!

Though he wanted to, Lew never legally adopted David—primarily out of consideration for his grandparents. In a letter Ellie wrote to Dave in 1990, she said,

> Joe lives on in you, and even in your offspring. You have his voice and especially his laugh, to go with the keen sense of humor. You stand the way he did—with your legs far apart as if to brace yourself. Once, a long time ago, I stood by his grave in Arlington National Cemetery and told him about you and how blessed we are in having Lew for a Dad and husband to care for us. Sometimes I even have this fantasy that God and Joe got together and sent your Dad to us. All through your growing up, Dad was there for you. Heredity is potentiality made active within an environment, they say. You had a father and a Dad and you are the best of them both.

A month before the wedding with Lew, on June 25, 1948, Joe's body was re-interred in Arlington Cemetery. Ellie wrote to Dave that she did not go to the ceremony and, while Momo and Popo were away, she burned all his letters in an incinerator—except one, she told me. There is something to be said about putting the past behind you in a thoughtful and positive way, and moving on.

Ellie did visit Joe's grave later, however. While Dad was at a golf tournament in Maryland when I was twelve years old and my brothers were at camp or working, Mom and I toured Washington. I vividly remember that she told me to stay in the car in Arlington Cemetery so she could be by herself. Now I know why.

Jack and I certainly knew about Joe from our earliest memories, and there were pictures of him in Momo's house. It was not a big deal that our older brother had a different last name; Momo and Popo Bainer were our grandparents too.

While Dad had was a boatload of relatives, Auntie "Lor" and "Howardnalice" (as we affectionately called them) were the only ones on Mom's side we knew. Auntie "Lor" was indeed formidable, calling us by our "Christian" names. She told "Eleanor" that my brother Jack's name sounded like a nightclub owner. (His proper name was John and that's what she called him; I was Stephen.) Jack later wrote a school essay about Auntie "Lor" as "His Most Unforgettable Character." Mom helped give him material. Auntie "Lor" died at the age of 90, alert and opinionated until the end, in a nursing home in Cleveland for women of a certain stature who had fallen on hard times.

So much had happened on Sunset Drive in the few years after it was constructed, and it would continue to play center stage of our family life. In 1955, the Davies Family of five traded our large Victorian house with a rental unit close to town with Momo and Popo's house on Sunset Drive. A boy had been hit by a car and killed in front of our house; Ellie thought it was David, for a moment. But it wasn't. That was the catalyst, but I think Momo also knew how much Ellie loved 435 Sunset, and wanted her all along to have a place with roots for the first time in her life. We loved Sunset Drive too, not just the house but the quintessential 1950s neighborhood full of kids, with brick streets leading to an abandoned stone quarry where you could build forts or hunt for polliwogs and salamanders.

Ellie and Lew did indeed live "happily ever after." It was a remarkable, fifty-five-year-long partnership—that's how they described it to others—of love, family, travel, business success, and community service. Surely my mother had earned this happiness, but her early years also prepared her for with dealing with loss, including eventually almost all of her contemporary friends who are all featured in this memoir. She found new, younger ones, though!

Our father had years of health challenges, too, before he died in 2003 at age eighty-five. Ellie was his loving caregiver through it all, and went on to live fully and resiliently, despite her own health issues, until she was nearly ninety-eight, passing away on Memorial Day weekend in 2017 after a bout of the flu. Her end was peaceful.

Ellie's rocky relationship with her sister did not improve. She cut off all ties with Ruth in the early 1950s after Ruth failed to pay her share of costs for her mother's funeral, dating back over a decade at that point. A collection agency came after Howard and Ellie. Ellie and Howard paid the funeral bill, but neither spoke to Ruth again, although they exchanged letters after Auntie "Lor" died. Howard—who moved to Los Angeles with Alice after the war and was Ellie's closest (and funniest) relative—said if she showed up at his house, he'd slam the door in her face. For Ellie, this separation was an act of protection, for even talking about Ruth would get her unnerved.

In the sanitarium, Ellie learned the value of finding time for herself. Throughout her life, she would take "mini-sanitariums" at elder hostels or country inns, where she would hole herself in, read, write, and recharge. Her interest in life-long learning was legendary. She was taking a class at Allegheny College a few months before she died, and the memoir itself was largely produced for classes she took and during her retreats, or when Dad would go away on business trips.

Her sister-in-law, Alice Hinig, wrote to her on what would have been her fiftieth anniversary to Joe Bainer: "Remembering your wedding, you looked so beautiful and radiant in your mother's dress. Howard looking handsome as he escorted you down the aisle to Joe, in his uniform and those wonderful boots! I know you loved him so—and he you. I wonder if your happiness with Joe prepared you for an especially good and joyous marriage with Lew. You give so much of yourself to your marriage—again I wonder if one happiness enables one to build on another."

Ellie never got around to writing about her second fifty years. My copy of her memoir, presented to the family for Christmas, is inscribed, "Done at last!" She was ninety-one and was not done in any sense of the word. Ellie was always looking forward: to the next adventure, the next opportunity for learning, the next person she could make her good friend—her "new beginnings"—even in her nineties. This was not something she was taught: she learned it the hard way by the time she was twenty-seven.

Sometime after Lew died in 2003, Ellie privately wrote a note to herself on one of those notepads she received from a charitable organization looking for a donation. She changed "A Note from Eleanor" to a "Note *to* Eleanor." I found it in her office after she died, filed in a folder called "Inspirations." It says, perceptively, "The challenge of losing a loved one is to honor his memory, while at the same time, that life moves forward so that only one person has died, not two. It's tough to move forward with life when you still long for the life you had. But there's no going back—so, go girl!"

And she did.

Stephen C. (Steve) Davies
September 30, 2019

Acknowledgements

This book is my mother's memoir and, if I could put myself in her shoes, I would say that she would have been ever so grateful to Lew, who encouraged her writing, and to her friends and family who appreciated and valued her accomplishments. Few have left such a legacy—written or otherwise—as Eleanor Curtis Hinig Bainer Davies.

As her "editor," let me begin by thanking my brothers and partners in Three Sons Press—Jack Davies and Kay Kendall and Dave and Linda Bainer—who encouraged and supported this project. Special thanks to Dave and Linda, who provided a large box of materials about Ellie's life with Joe Bainer that she had given them. Thanks go also to my good friend and accomplished editor David Grogan who made important early recommendations and to Annah MacKenzie who was invaluable in helping me edit and organize the story, while preserving Ellie's original voice. Gail Berg escorted me around Cleveland Heights and Shaker Heights so we could photograph all of houses featured in this book. It was quite an adventure! Other friends (conveniently visiting my house in Chautauqua, New York) assisted as well, including Judy Merryman who came out of retirement briefly and used her considerable graphic design talents to produce the book cover. Barbara Taylor, Connie Moffit, and cousin Marion Nesbit proved to be eagle-eyed proofreaders. And deep appreciation goes to my cousin, Allison Girvin, a journalist who was very close to her Great Aunt Ellie. Allison helped me more fully conceive this book while sitting on my porch in Chautauqua in the summer of 2018 and critiqued the early drafts as we both concluded that, yes, indeed, Ellie had a book.